RUDE BUAY

Original Story ...
By
International
Bestselling Author
John A. Andrews

The RUDE BUAY Series®

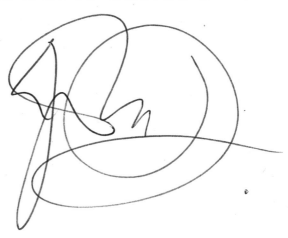

RUDE BUAY

... The Unstoppable

aka Rude Boy ... The Unstoppable

by

International

Bestselling Author

John A. Andrews

Other Titles Include:

Dare To Make A Difference — Success 101 For Teens

Total Commitment - The Mindset of Champions

When The Dust Settles - A True Hollywood Story

How I Wrote 8 Books In One Year

Whose Woman Was She?

The FIVE "Ps" For Teens

Who Shot The Sheriff?

Cross Atlantic Fiasco

A Snitch On Time

Quotes Unlimited

L.A. Undercover

Agent O'Garro

N Y C

RUDE BUAY

Published in the U.S.A. by
Books That Will Enhance Your Life™

A L I - Andrews Leadership International
Entertainment Division®
Jon Jef Jam Entertainment®

Cover Design: John A. Andrews
Cover Graphic Designer:John Andrews/Abhai Kaul
Cover Photo: Anthony Johnson
Edited by: Pernell Marsh/ALI
ISBN: 978-0-983-1419-52

Table Of Contents

"Ask not what your country can do for you - ask what you can do for your country."
- John F. Kennedy

1

A CUPBOARD DOOR SLAMS SHUT!

"What's taking you so long to pack your bag, boy? You are going to be late for school again, the second day in a row Randy." That parental voice came screaming from the kitchen and echoing upstairs through Randy's untidy room. Randy in a state of urgency forces his tattered notebooks inside his one strap, still hanging book bag.

"Mom I got it, will you stop screaming at me?"

ONE YEAR LATER:

All lights are out except the one in Rude Buay's room.
He lies on his back studying from a grease-stained
book by candlelight. The Officer walks by and notices.
With a vindictive look he opens up the door, and in
thick patois dialect, he confronts Randy. "That is
murder you know, me na know way dem ah talk bout
when dem say it's only manslaughter. You wicked
mon! Him ah me sister's son, her only begotten. Bend
over!" He retrieves a twisted switch and whips Randy
across his backside several times. Randy cries out,
"I did not push your nephew. He slipped! "
Another prisoner across the way witnesses and yells
out at the Officer, "Leave the boy alone, mon! The law
is the law whether you live on a hill or inside tenement
yard."
The Officer discontinues his brutal attack on Randy,
puts out the light, confiscates the book, and
extinguishes the candle.
Randy staggers to get up off the floor and onto the bed.
He's bruised so badly, blood trickles down backside
and forearms.

SIX YEARS LATER:

Randy's older brother Clifford on his way home was
confronted by several drug dealers outside the

perimeter of their tenement yard. He tried eluding the Uzi wielding quartet but they had him cornered. The leader of the pack yells, "This is our turf, you are hurting our revenue."

Clifford, arguably replied, "I and I live here! I sell what and where I want."

Gunshots like popcorn ring out from their weapons, as they cut Clifford down, leaving him blood-drenched on the sidewalk.

Several tenement dwellers rush to the scene as the supped up green, yellow, and black Mustang speeds away.

A woman wearing an oil-stained apron and carrying a large kitchen fork yells out. "Miss Bascombe, its Clifford! They shot up Clifford bad, mon."

Randy and his mom abort dinner at the dinner table and rush to the scene. She pushes through the gathered crowd towards her son Clifford.

Trying to comfort him, she's now immersed with his blood. His limp hands and body, indicate his life-lessness.

Randy, bathed in tears, looks on.

A Jamaican police land Rover pulls up. Two officers jump out and proceed with their investigation. Several tenement dwellers retreat because of police presence. The senior officer in his 50s asks, "Any witnesses?" as the junior officer releases Miss Bascombe's tight grasp on Clifford. Simultaneously he notices the kitchen fork in a woman's hand. The woman pointing up the street with the fork yells out in deep patois, "Mustang, the color of the flag! You all better find them…"

The officer interrupts.

"Miss, my name is officer Lent. What is your name?"

The woman now with her fork holding hand on her hip responds.

"Maude! Maude Davis."

Maude Davis, what you are holding in your hand is considered a deadly weapon."

She continues, "Worry bout me officer Lent, and let the murderers go free, instead of fighting crime you are fighting me. Shoo, fire ah go burn you." And she moseys inside the tenement yard, leaving Randy and his mother to complete the police report.

ONE MONTH LATER:

Before daybreak, a taxi pulls up outside the tenement yard and waits. The only illuminated dwellings belong to Miss Bascombe and Maude Davis. Suddenly, the light at the Bascombe's dwelling goes out. Miss Bascombe locks her door and follows Randy in tow as he knocks on Maude's door with a suitcase and a carryon bag in hand. Maude comes to the door and embraces him.

"Take care of yourself Rude Buay. I will look after your mother for you."

Randy replies gratefully, "Thanks Godmother, I'll miss you." The car horn honks. He continues, "The cab is waiting." He departs and enters the cab accompanied by his mom.

Later, he stands amongst travelers at Michael Manley International Airport and embraces his mom in tears. Then swiftly Randy heads towards the American Airlines departure lounge waving goodbye.

2

ARRIVING IN NEW YORK, Randy Bascombe acquired a job as a parking attendant, while he figured out exactly what he wanted to do with his life. He was determined to put the imprisoned past behind him.

Deep in his psyche, he knew that he wanted to fight crime. However, becoming a police officer, he would be a mediocre accomplishment. Plus, he tragically witnessed firsthand, the ineptness of that entity, when his brother was shot and killed by drug dealers. That Jamaican tragedy stood out like a sore thumb.

He worked hard during the week, and on weekends, he frequented the library.

Before 1960 Americans did not use drugs as acceptable behavior. Neither did Randy Bascombe, who was born after that era. He saw it as a serious offense. Additionally, losing his brother in a drug-related incident contributed to his abstinence.

Randy gravitated to materials dealing with drug enforcement. He was very much taken aback, when he read the stats that DEA Special Agents grew from 1,470 in 1973 to 2,135 in 1975, two years later.

Retrospectively, his present, once quiet neighborhood, where he played street basketball, was now saturated with drug dealers, buyers, pimps and prostitutes.

This growing Law Enforcement entity became more and more attractive to him. Consequently, he not only studied up on what the U.S. was doing to fight the war on drugs but got so immersed in the subject that he decided to attend college.

There he earned a bachelor's degree, majoring in Criminal Justice and Police Science. Randy came clean on his background check among other requirements. Coincidentally, the Jamaican authorities had recently cleared him from manslaughter charges as a kid. Judge Hastings had revisited the case and found him innocent of the charges.

Randy Bascombe, felt like a new man when he received the phone call that he was hired as a Drug Enforcement

Agent. Bascombe, left New York for Virginia, where he underwent basic training. Upon completing this process, he looked at several major cities where he would like to work. Miami and New York were his top choices, but to give the other cities an equal chance, he included their names in a hat, closed his eyes and drew one. He picked Miami, Florida. To him this was a perfect choice for two reasons:

(1) Miami was close to Jamaica, and it would only take a few hours to hop on a plane and visit his Mom and Maude Davis.

(2) His graduating class all wanted to work for Special Agent Bob White. Why? White, was not only highly-skilled, but he was an intuitive, motivated, and deeply committed agent.

So, Bascombe was interviewed and joined the DEA in Miami. Sadly though, after only being under Bob White's tutelage for two months, White was executed during a friendly fire incident. His assistant, Jose Mendez, was appointed to "fill his shoes."

3

MRS. BLACK, a middle-aged history teacher, collects the last batch of test papers from her students. She places the stack on her desk and reminds the students to be back in their seats immediately after the lunch break. The school bell rings.

Ray, a skinny teenager, shows his disgust with her request. He darts out of the classroom and rushes through the crowded schoolyard. Chattering kids mingle. In the distance, Ray makes a break across the street, to the local grocery store.

Moments later, dozens of kids assemble in the L-shaped cafeteria enjoying their lunch. A variety of food odors fills the air. On the outside, Ray appears. He is larger than life, demonstrative by a hard-wine interlude. Many kids follow suit in the revelry. The revelry expands and intensifies as it progresses inside the cafeteria.

Teens, enjoying their lunch, would rather not participate in the carousing. But indulge in food tossing attack on the boisterous intruders. Fighting back, their partying turns into the displaying of their food tossing skills.

Two security guards abandon catching up on the sports scores in the Jamaican Gleaner and rush to the scene. After their intense, wielding of the batons, the kids are subdued. Many leave the scene, while the sane ones stay behind and clean up the food residue.

A few yards away, Ray and many of his partying buddies huddle. Their voices are inaudible. A chain reaction, vicious, skin scratching dilemma begins. Rashes break out on their face and hands. Uncontrollably, they begin falling onto the school grounds. Some kids tough it out.

Teachers, students, as well as increased school security personnel, rush in an attempt to investigate and comfort the ailing kids. The persistent ones are now gasping for air and eventually fall to the ground. The fallen attack the sympathetic cries of their classmates, other students, and school personnel alike. Mrs. Black emerges on the scene terrified.

Ray, lies in a fetal position, biting hard into the unpaved school grounds. His classmates and teacher, hover, puzzled; they can't believe what has transpired since the bell rang. The next bell rings, some students saunter back to the classroom; others remain to bathe in grief.

The sound of sirens can be heard in the distance. The increase in decibels indicates their closeness. Suddenly, ambulances pull up. The schoolyard is now a spectacle of flashing lights, cries, and flashing lights. Medics rush out, wheeling stretchers. The debilitated teens are placed on them and rushed inside ambulances, one at a time.

Jamaican Police vehicles emerge onto the scene. Officers jump out and investigate. They carefully collect food residue off the ground and deposit it into trash bags.

Meanwhile, inside the principal's office, terrified teachers congregate. They rummage through the backpacks of ailing kids. Contents are emptied onto the principal's desk. Tiny, neat packets in aluminum foil, along with textbooks, fall from a midnight blue backpack onto the desk bearing the name Ray C. The two overworked security guards, overseeing the search, unwrap one of the packages. Inside, one of the guards discovers a white powdery substance. He refolds it and places it along with the other unopened ones, inside a brown envelope. He seals it airtight. The on-looking teachers wail hysterically, as a result of the findings.

Two officers, wearing transparent gloves, enter and confiscate the envelope. After which they rush to their cruiser, and drive away speedily.

In the meantime, medics steer gurneys with bodies wrapped in white sheets to the morgue at the general hospital. Dozens of tagged bodies (reading Cyanide Overdose) are transported inside this small rectangular-shaped facility. Ray Collins' body makes its way in, followed by his breathless mother, bawling and engulfed in tears. Wearing a soiled dress, with an apron tied around her waist, a multi-colored head tie blowing in the wind, she carries her shoes in her hand. Other parents, in search of their kids, embrace one another in tears. The busy medics sense their grief.

4

THOUSANDS OF MILES AWAY in Bogota, Columbia, livestock graze noisily behind a warehouse. From the hills above, clouds of dust rise from between the trees. The dust follows in tow of a moving object. That yellow hummer speeding through the bushes finally reveals itself, as it emerges and comes to a bumpy, screeching halts.

Immediately, three women jump out:

First, beautiful dark-skinned Agnes Richards. She is in her late 20s, wearing unkempt braids, and carrying two black duffel bags. Second, Asian, trophy woman, Denise Gomez. She is in her late 20s. Denise carries a duffel bag over her shoulder and a semi-automatic rifle in the other. The huge diamond stone on her ring kissing her wedding band glitters in the sun as she kisses her wedding band. She's all business. Following Denise is a tall, feisty, WWE type, Shelly Hall. A Caucasian in her early 30s. She sports a ponytail hairstyle, and totes two larger duffel bags in one hand. On the other, a semi-automatic rifle. She proceeds in tow of her two traveling partners.

Denise gives them a wink, then leads the way to the shack. The livestock disperses as she moves up to the steel door of the shack. Denise enters a code. The door unlocks. She pulls it open. The three women enter in haste and quickly load up duffel bags with packages containing about five kilos each, labeled: DRAGON X. They load up their hummer and drives away, leaving a trail of dust behind.

Back in Jamaica, outside the general hospital, the sounds of sirens fill the air. Ambulances eventually show their presence. Now idle, with lights still flashing, the paramedics wheel gurneys out, towards several, excessively, vomiting kids. One paramedic, sporting an elongated dreadlocks hairstyle, wheels a teen, who is foaming extensively through the nose inside the ER.

Upon entering, the paramedic glances at the kid and announces:

"This one stopped breathing!"

He checks for a pulse, there is none. He quickly administers CPR. He pauses. Then echoes: 'Nothing! We lost her."

Sirens are heard in the distance, as emerging ambulances raced to the scene. Police vehicles join the emergency response units.

Mourners crowd the ER entrance. Their cries increase in decibels, sandwiched by deep patois, transcending into an inaudible lamentation. So much, that it competes with the ambulance siren.

Jamaican police, rush from an occupied gurney after occupied gurney, with pen and clipboard, collecting data.

Meanwhile, in Columbia, a twin-engine plane taxis as the yellow hummer races towards it. The aircraft speeds up and takes off to the sky, blanketing the vehicle with dust.

In the interim, in a downtown Bogota hotel, Axel James, sits on a couch smoking a long marijuana spliff. He is of Columbian decent, in his mid-forties. Axel displays the tattoo of a dragon below his right ear lobe and has a missing index finger and expensive gold rings on the four fingers of his right hand.

Ricardo Herrera, also of Columbian decent, in his mid-thirties, robust in demeanor, sitting across from Axel James, cogitates. Behind his right earlobe, Ricardo sports the same signature as Axel.

In walks, Ian Baynes, African American, in his late thirties: he is dressed in a pilot's uniform, horned rimmed glasses. The handle of his glasses almost kissing his dragon tattoo. Ian faces Axel but dares not

"Calm down sisters. Let me explain," remarks Axel James.

Agnes responds, "No time for your explanation. Our clients are waiting. The last shipment was laced with cyanide. People are dying, Axel."

Ricardo creates a decoy. Denise refocuses.

"That's not the way we do business. Clients wait until the goods are delivered. X label was a glitch," states Ricardo.

'We paid in advance!" says Shelly as she aims at Ricardo's head.

Axel James interjects, "We are trying to bring in a fresh shipment into Port Antonio. One is already on its way, just give it time."

Denise eyeballs him while she caresses the trigger on her rifle.

"No one informed me about the crap you sent us. Now picking up in Port Antonio would create a nightmare. Too many sniffing MP'S." Denise states.

"That's right. You've.." says Agnes.

"Time is our money, Axel." Denise reminds him.

Looking at Denise, he responds. "Your husband's aware of the delay. His business in Miami is hurting... Meet us in Montego Bay tomorrow morning. We'll be covering all of our tracks."

Axel, Ian, and Ricardo board the red pickup truck and drive off.

The three women withdraw their arms, jump inside Hummer, and depart unhappily.

5

AT THE DRUG ENFORCEMENT AGENCY in Miami,
Special Agent Jose Mendez, in his late forties, lights up
a cigar. He then hands over a set of keys to agent
Randy Bascombe and departs. Bascombe, nicknamed
RUDE BUAY aka "Rude Boy" is of Jamaican descent
and in his early forties. He's adorned with a scorpion
tattooed to his bald head, with fangs upstaging his
forehead and tail extending towards his right earlobe.
Bascombe familiarizes himself with the surroundings.
He removes a portrait of Jamaica from a box, hangs it
on the wall, and stares at it retrospectively. Next, he
retrieves a portrait of his older brother. Reminisced by
the picture, he fumbles. The portrait falls. He catches it
before it hits the ground. He takes in a second look.

The office phone rings. He lays the portrait securely on top of his desk, before answering.

The voice in the phone states, "Requesting DEA presence at the corner of Main and Broadway."

Bascombe picks his brother's portrait off his desk and hangs it securely on the wall. He throws on his jacket over his strapped two semiautomatics and heads out, hitting the streets.

Bascombe pulls up on Broadway and waits. A red Monte Carlo is parked on Main. A rugged-looking, Hispanic Man, in his mid-thirties, comes out of the high rise office building on Broadway. He's carrying an attaché case. Bascombe gets out of his car in a calculated pursuit. The Man gets inside the hot rod. Bascome, on foot, is catching up to him. The Man attempts to stick the key into the ignition. Bascombe sticks his left hand through the driver's window, grabbing at the keys. Bascombe fails to grab the keys, but the suspect rolls up the electronic window, putting Bascombe's hand in a vice.

The car takes off. Bascombe tries to keep pace with the speeding car. The Man looks at Bascombe's trapped hand and laughs hysterically. The Monte Carlo turns a corner, throwing Bascombe's body onto the hood. His hand is still fastened. He manages to viciously shoot at the suspect through the windshield using his other hand, at the suspect. An oncoming tractor-trailer honks, as it closes in on the Monte-Carlo, now zig-zagging over the yellow line. Before the trailer could clip Bascombe, the Man shoots at Bascombe's trapped hand and blows out the driver's side window. Bascombe is thrown free onto the sidewalk. The car slams into a telephone pole.

The man crawls out on the passenger side, bloodied and shaken up, yet, he escapes on foot. The trailer proceeds, regardless.

Bascombe, incurs several lacerations to his face, head, along with minor bruises over some parts of his body. In pain, he gets up, puts two fingers in his mouth and whistles in an attempt to stop an oncoming taxi cab. His whistle is inaudible. The cab passes him by. Moments later, an ambulance arrives and whisks him away.

Meanwhile, Shelly, Agnes, and Denise embarking on their Jamaican quest board a Jamaican taxi cab, occupying the rear seat. The driver, adjusts his rearview mirror, attempting to eavesdrop.

Shelly declares, "We're going to MO BAY airport. Could you get us there in fifteen?"

Driver nods, yes.

The taxi turns in the opposite direction. Shelly notices. "Where...are you going?" she asks.

"Shortcut," replies the cab driver.

"I don't like shortcuts!" Shelly echoes.

The driver makes another turn and swings into a driveway. The three women are frustrated, as they feel cornered.

Immediately, the taxi stops. Abandoned vehicles create a spectacle. Axel James emerges from behind an abandoned car. He has a black bag in one hand and a gun in the other.

"Do not get out of the car," he commands.

In dismay, Shelly looks at the cab driver, then back at Axel.

"Where is our merchandise? Con Man!" Shelly asks, demandingly.

Axel inches towards the cab. The cab driver, fearing a shootout, exits the cab.

Axel is distracted. Shelly swings the front passenger door open, it hits Axel hard, and knocks the gun completely out of his hand.

The three women jump out with switchblades in confrontation, before Axel can retrieve his gun. Axel is trapped. Ian Baynes, sensing a bloody end to his boss, comes to his aid.

Pointing his gun at the three women. Ian exclaims, "Not so fast ladies."

Shelly tosses her knife at Axel James. He dodges. The knife misses him and lodges in the board behind him. Axel grabs the knife by its handle, flings it back at Shelly. She ducks. As a result, the knife sails through the taxi's rear window and lodges in the seat.

Shelly comes at Axel with a left uppercut. He ducks. She returns with a left uppercut. Again, he ducks out of it. This time, he grabs her hand and twists it behind her back.

Following up, he whacks her hard in the face. Shelly staggers and falls to the ground.

Witnessing the manhandling of Shelly pisses off Denise. Frustrated, she yells, "Where's our product, Axel?"

Axel James points to the black bag on the ground. Agnes picks the bag up, opens it. Satisfied, she throws it inside the taxi. Finally, Shelly gets up and crawls in on the other side of the cab.

Ricardo, taking no chances, keeps his gun pointed at Denise. Ian Baynes, sensing water under the bridge, returns to the car. Axel, signals "let's go" to Ricardo.

The taxi driver, observes from a distance. Axel, while departing, looks over at him authoritatively. "Take those bitches to the airport!" he commands.

The driver nervously walks over to his taxi. He gets in. Agnes and Denise get in. The taxi drives off.

Axel, Ricardo, and Ian witnessing their peaceful departure enter their car and take off in the opposite direction.

The taxi travels speedily through the potholed streets of Montego Bay. Shelly wipes her face and stares at her blood-stained hands.

"I have to piss. Driver, can you pull over?"

He complies.

"Now get out of the car,"

Shelly commands.

He tries to grab the car keys.

Shelly opens her switchblade and stabs him once. He manages to open the door, exiting the cab. She gets out in pursuit. Shelly stabs him several times. He crouches, falls to the ground, kicks around and stops breathing. Shelly, gathers some leaves, cleans the blade. She looks at it. Noticing blood residue, she cleans it thoroughly with her red bandana, after which, she takes the wheel.

6

LATER, AGNES, SHELLY, AND DENISE dressed to the nines, all emerge from the ladies room at Montego Bay Airport. Their sensualistic physique grabs attention, as their oversized "rack" giggles. Shelly holds on carefully to that black bag recovered from Axel.

A luscious hottie, exquisitely outfitted, Jamaican style, joins them as they meander through customs all toting duffel bags. A Caucasian businessman, traveling in the opposite direction, is distracted by the estrogenic aura. He smashes into a pillar, sending his carry-ons flying. Embarrassingly he recovers but finds himself blanketed by the crowd he attracted.

Hours later, the American Airlines 747 touches down in Miami, Florida. The aircraft comes to a complete stop, but its doors remain closed.

A U.S. Marshall steps out of the cockpit and forms a huddle with two flight attendants. Sage Ross, in her late twenties, is as sophisticated as they come. Her Ivy League status shows through in her communication skills. Sean Williams, in his late thirties, listens attentively. The Marshall glances at Agnes, who grabs his attention, in so many different ways. He compartmentalizes his thoughts and then refocuses.

"She fits the description...conveyed to us by Jamaican police," states the U.S. Marshall.

"What do we do?" asks Sage.

Meanwhile, Denise seductively applies hot red lipstick. A passenger across the aisle devours a pack of multi-colored M and M's.

"Keep the passengers in their seats. Bring in the DEA."

Sage picks up the microphone. With an air of sophistication, she announces:

"Thanks for flying American Airlines flight 1934. When the aircraft comes to a stop, we ask that you please remain in your seats for further instructions."

Sage enters the cockpit as the aircraft comes to a stop. Passengers panic, in a state of restlessness, mainly those four women in question.

The Hottie, sitting behind Denise, reaches inside her pocketbook and pulls out an object. She quickly removes the rubberized casing, revealing a "Dillinger." She shoots at the Marshall. The bullet misses him, hits a passing male flight attendant, who falls on top of several passengers. She shoots again.

The agile Marshall moves and the round grazes his shoulder, ricochets and penetrates the plane's skin. Marshall returns fire and shoots her in the face.

Passengers are screaming, some of them swearing. Denise, Agnes, and Shelly rummage nervously through their carry-on luggage under the seat. They cleverly remove a package each. Unnoticed by everyone else they place their luggage under their seats, behind other luggage. The Marshall, surveying, steps over the dead body in the aisle, then returns to the cockpit area.

Two concerned pilots, now concerned more than ever, remain seated at the controls. Sage dials.

The Marshall, somewhat annoyed with himself, exclaims,

"She's dead."

He fetches the phone in front of the cockpit and dials.

On the desk of DEA Bascombe, a pen phone rings. No one is there. In the office, the wall is displayed portraits of Jamaica. Agent Bascombe's nameplate stands out amongst the stacks of folders on his desk. The phone continues to ring.

Inside the green room, Bascombe fetches a cup of coffee and leaves the green room with a cup of coffee in hand. He accidentally spills some of the drinks on his suit and tie. Yet, he pays no attention to the spillage. He's got a more urgent task - getting to the phone.

He grabs the pen phone that's been ringing unremittingly.

"Hello, this is agent Randy Bascombe!"

In speaker mode, he listens in as he writes with his pen phone.

"Okay. No one gets off that plane! "

He dials on the device.

Agent Desmond Scott, Caucasian, good looking stud, in his mid-thirties, aborts the name search on the computer. He picks up the call.

"Scott, this is agent Bascombe. Meet me outside with the black Tahoe, ready to go."

Scott dashes out.

Bascombe dials again.

Heidi Hudson, Caucasian, in her late twenties, aborts applying her makeup and picks up.

"Agent Hudson, we need you on this..."

She jumps up, checks her gun. Satisfied, she darts out. Bascombe inspects his tie. He goes to his locker. He opens it. Inside the locker, there's a sports coat that matches his pants. He removes his jacket and tie, hangs them in the locker, puts on the sports coat, and takes off as a man possessed. He turns doorknob to Mendez's office. The door is locked. Bascombe dashes out towards the lobby. There, he bumps into Mendez, knocking the box of Kentucky Fried Chicken to the ground. Bascombe regains his balance. Mendez picks up the box of KFC.

"Yet another wild goose chase?" he asks.

"This is huge. Dade County Airport." Responds Randy Bascombe.

"Aren't you supposed to check with me first?" asks Mendez.

Bascombe, glancing at the box of KFC in Jose Mendez's hand, replies.

"Sorry..."

Mendez, focusing on Bascombe, asks:

"Who's the informant?"

Bascombe reflects, and then replies, "American Airlines. The flight originated in Jamaica."

Heidi Hudson barges in. She stares inquisitively at Bascombe and Special agent Mendez. She readily arranges her hair into a ponytail.

"Are we going to the Caribbean?" she asks smilingly.

Bascombe is focused. He addresses Mendez.

Chief...

Mendez interrupts him.

"I know. I'll be sending you some needed backup."

Outside, the Black Tahoe emerges from the parking structure and stops abruptly. Desmond Scott is at the wheel.

Bascombe jumps in the front passenger seat. Agent Hudson scurries in the rear seat and reaches for the seat belt.

"So where are we heading?" asks agent Hudson.

The Tahoe takes off. Agent Hudson accidentally loses her balance.

Bascombe, with a delayed response.

"Dade County Airport!"

"Who's involved?" she asks.

Bascombe overwhelmed with her questions.

"Step on it, Scott. One woman, there could be more."

Meanwhile, inside the aircraft. Shelly, tries to switch another passenger's bag with hers.

Seth, a flaming guy, catches her in the act.

"Did you just move my bag?" he yells.

"I'm sorry, it looked like mine." Shelly remarks.

"Don't be sorry. Can't you read? It says SETH!"

"Bitch, I said I'm sorry." Replies Shelly.

She sits back down clutching on to her carry on.

Seth, not trusting her, gets up and examines his bag. Opening it, he discovers two pieces of silicone, stuffed with small zip-locked packages. Staring at Shelly's reduced "rack". Seth erupts,

"Help! This bitch is trying to frame me. You've got the wrong man..."

He removes both objects from his bag and holds them in his hand. Treating them as a personal object, he draws an audience.

"This is a "D" cup." Seth removes the packages from the silicone.

Meanwhile, the Tahoe pulls up outside the aircraft. Agents, armed, ready to shoot, rush towards aircraft.

Back inside, Shelly removes herself from that seat and sits in an empty seat a few rows back.

The Marshall returning from the cockpit with a log intercedes.

Seth, still obsessed with the fake breast gently lays them on Shelly's empty seat.

Agents, now on board huddle with Sage along with the Marshall reviewing the passenger's log. The Marshall points to the three women and Shelly's fake breasts on the seat. Hudson eyes the pieces of silicone, perturbed. Bascombe, commands: "My name is agent Randy Bascombe - Miami Drug Enforcement Agency. Shelly Hall, Denise Gomez, and Agnes Richards, you are under arrest for alleged drug possession. Come to the front of the aircraft with your hands on top of your head."

The women, reluctantly cooperate.

Bascombe, place them in handcuffs. The other agents swarm the aircraft collecting their carryon.

Outside the abandoned aircraft, more Police vehicles converge, including a Coroner's vehicle. The three handcuffed women are pushed inside of a police utility vehicle. The vehicle drives to outside Dade County Prison. The women are escorted inside the prison and booked by Miami police officers.

7

IN KINGSTON, JAMAICA, festive music is playing. Pedestrians crowd the busy streets in a dancing mood. Busy vendors display merchandise, enticing tourists to shop. One tourist walks up to a vendor and window shop. Every style of hat under the sun is stocked. The tourist cleverly slips him a U.S. Twenty dollar bill. The Vendor takes it in his left hand, and sticks out his right, asking for more. The tourist opens his wallet, hands him another twenty. The vendor discretely hands him a brown bag. The tourist surveys his surroundings and secures it inside his pocket. He proceeds up the street. A Teen enjoys some fresh cotton candy as he helps a blind man cross the street. Voluptuous women parade the streets, creating a "turn on" to the men enjoying the view.

A Taxi pulls up. Two Hotties with oversized tanks (breast) jump inside. The cab takes off.

The Teen, making a B-line, dashes out of its way to avoid getting run over by the taxi.

Meanwhile, in the cab, the indulging cabby gets an eyeful in the rearview mirror.

Suddenly, he asks the passengers,

"Where do you, two bumptious women..., "

The taller of the two responds."

"University of the West Indies, West Kingston. Hurry!" The Cabby "steps on it" while he scans the radio station. He finds the right music to compliment the vibe and personalizes "Sweet Jamaica" in a sweet baritone voice.

The song ends, another starts. He searches for the right key to this ballad and gets it.

"This is our stop!" announces the Hottie.

The Taxi pulls up to the curb and stops outside a booth, with a variety of merchandise on display. Two women of less voluptuousness step out of booth, and trade places with the two Hotties. The cab takes off.

Moments later, teenagers flock the booth in droves, like flies to molasses. They are eager, to purchase the white powdery substance, in a transparent wrap. The teen, previously helping the blind man across the street, shows up breathless, pays for his packet and smilingly opens it.

One of the Hotties gets into a taxi. Later, it pulls up next to a closed grocery store. The Hottie jumps out and slides a large envelope underneath the door. She returns to the waiting taxi. It takes off.

An approaching police cruiser with flashing lights pursues the taxi. The taxi pulls over and stops curbside. Without hesitating, the Hottie jumps out and shoots at two approaching officers. One is hit, he falls to the ground. The other officer shoots back, striking the Hottie, she collapses and falls to the ground. She dies instantly. The Officer attends to his partner, who is still breathing. Sirens in the distance accompany a blanket of pedestrians, now converged onto the bloody scene.

8

A TEACHER HURRIES through the school gate and boards the waiting airport bus, with a folder in hand. She closes the door securely, after entering. Two women disguised as tour guides emerge from the back of the bus. The Teacher hands over the folder to them. They quickly scan through the folder and conduct a careful headcount. They present the folder to the Bus Driver. His dragon tattoo behind his right ear lobe is very revealing. He conceals the folder.

The Women reach into their aprons and pull out several fist-sized aluminum foil packets resembling those recovered from Ray's backpack. These packets are quickly distributed to each kid, along with a bottle of bottled water and a sheet of instructions.

The anxious kids review the instruction pamphlets and then consume the packets, aided by water. The bus pulls into a small airport-hanger. A twin-engine jet with propellers turning in slow motion - waits. The kids are transferred to that waiting aircraft.

Back in Miami, at the DEA Headquarters, Bascombe paces, while Mendez sits at the desk smoking a cigar.

Bascombe, perturbed, throws the newspaper onto the desk. He composes himself, facing Mendez squarely and addresses him.

"I would like to put in my request for an early vacation."

Jose Mendez asks:

"Family...?" As if he is not up to speed on the current fiasco in Jamaica.

Bascombe, feeling as if his intelligence has been insulted, remarks,

"No one seems to be doing anything about all these kids dying off like flies in Jamaica."

Mendez reassures.

"I am sure their government is handling that situation."

Bascombe, not giving up:

"Their MP's could be in on this whole fiasco."

Mendez responds,

"They've already imprisoned the Drug Lords. That's progress!"

Bascombe reflects.

"My mom used to always say "There's more in the Marta besides the pestle"

Mendez, understanding the cliché, comments,

"Do you think there's more to it? I think you should let

the government do their job. They are ..."

Suddenly, the four eyes in that room are glued to the TV set, as a news reporter interrupts the scheduled program.

"Late-breaking news, as we continue to follow this fiasco in Jamaica. The death toll continues to rise as three teenagers died today as a result of using cyanide-laced cocaine. One drug dealer, a woman, was also shot and killed by Jamaican police. As a result of this shoot out, one officer has been hospitalized. The death toll equals ninety."

Mendez, to it all, responds.

"Everyone seems to be using the "F" word way too much - FIASCO."

Bascombe, in disbelief, (concerning his boss's attitude), goes to the window. Reflecting, he looks outside.

Bascombe retreats.

Before further addressing Mendez, he points to his brother's portrait on the wall.

"My only sibling. Lost him in a drug-related incident."

Mendez, nods, indicating that all that is old news. Then he remarks,

"My condolences..."

Bascombe has endured enough.

"I refuse to let more of relatives go through this fiasco. If not now? When? Some innocent person's kid is going to be next. That is my final "F" word." Bascombe throws the keys on the desk at Mendez and walks out of the office.

Mendez gets up from his seat at Bascombe's desk and takes in a close up view of the portrait for the first time. Moments later, Mendez moseys up behind Bascombe in the Green Room. Bascombe, adding cream to his coffee, sees him peripherally. Mendez apologetically returns the keys to agent Bascombe. Scott and Hudson surprise them, by barging in during the reconciliation. Mendez bids farewell to Agent Desmond Scott and Agent Heidi Hudson. The three agents board a Miami Police SUV with their luggage in tow.

9

THE 747 AIRPLANE touches down at Michael Manley Airport in Jamaica. Agents Bascombe, Scott, and Hudson move briskly through the crowded Jamaican airport terminal. Outside the terminal, the agents hustle toward the blue unmarked police vehicle, waiting. A Distinguished Gentleman, dressed in white attire steps out. He hands over the keys to Bascombe, along with a folded piece of paper. Bascombe reads the address: The Villa, 23 Pine Grove, St. Andrew, Jamaica. Before getting inside, Bascombe asks.

"Is this thing GPS equipped?"

The Gentleman, replies,

"Rude Buay, it has recently been installed in our entire fleet. On the other hand, I must tell you that the Jamaican government is not very happy with your involvement."

Bascombe replies.

"I understand. Dual citizenship has its advantages. Doesn't it?"

The Gentleman continues,

"How about your team?"

Heidi Hudson, interjects.

"Where agent Bascombe goes, we go!"

"A dual name does have its disadvantage, agent Bascombe. I'm sorry, RUDE BUAY. Anyway, your brother will appreciate this homecoming." The Gentleman admonishes.

Rude Buay, looks towards heaven.

Heidi Hudson admires the gentleman. He then makes the sign of the cross and smilingly gives Rude Buay thumbs up. The Agents jump inside the vehicle. The Distinguished Gentleman departs and moseys inside the terminal as their car takes off.

It's a great distance from the airport to the Villa. Agent Bascombe takes control of the car along the winding roads of Kingston, en-route to Mandeville.

A beautiful, Victorian designed house, with an earthen extended driveway, nestles on the hill above homes of lesser value.

Rude Buay brings the car to a stop. With Hudson covering him, they move in, weapons drawn. Scott waits outside the car, armed and ready.

Rude Buay and Hudson arrive closer toward the house. They scrutinize their surroundings. Feeling satisfied, Rude Buay inches closer towards the front door. He kicks the door in and charges inside, with agent Hudson in tow.

Now inside, both agents proceed intensely, but with immense caution. Their entrance has them staring into a sunken living room, with a giant screen TV, a black leather couch and a huge glass center table. On the table, the neatly folded maps get their attention momentarily, but they remain focused.

Commandingly, Rude Bauy cautions.

"US drug enforcement agents! Come out nice and slow with your hands on top of your head."

There is no response. A black Cat emerges. Rude Buay releases the safety on his gun. The cat meows. Hudson, now standing over the center table, gets a closer look at the contents. She notices three separate sets of maps of the Jamaican city of Port Antonio.

Next to the maps lay syringes on a tray, straws, a crack pipe, two cigarette lighters, and cocaine residue, validating the habits of the dwellers.

Rude Buay's attention is drawn to several pieces of luggage in a corner. However, he proceeds into the room where the cat exited. Agent Hudson proceeds into the other room while covering Rude Buay from the corner of her eyes.

Rude Buay rummages through the room. He cautiously checks a closet, as he slowly pulls the door open. It's empty. He throws off the bed mattress and box spring. He checks under the bed; nothing's underneath it. On the nightstand, he notices a replica of "The Tempest," a beautiful yacht. Rude Buay admires it.

Hudson's voice penetrates the room.

"Rude Buay! You've got to see this."

Rude Buay, with a gun, still drawn, vacates that room and joins her.

In the second bedroom, Agent Hudson stands in front of a giant-sized closet with its door ajar. She proceeds to rid it of its contents. Packets labeled: Dragon X, attache' cases, guns, stacks of Jewish bankrolls in various currency, grenades and survival kits, put things in perspective. Rude Buay and Hudson more committed than ever to the manhunt, continue rummaging through the house.

In Jamaican prison, a rat runs across the entrance to cell number fifteen and disappears. Axel James, dressed in prison garb, stares in the direction of the disappearing creature.

In the meantime, outside the prison, a Black sedan rolls up. Ricardo and Ian Baynes, dressed in prison security uniforms, step out and hasten through a huge iron gate.

An on-duty Security Guard, sitting in the booth, acknowledges them with a nod of the head. They proceed into the interior of the prison.

Back at the booth, a new Guard replaces the on-duty guard.

Inside the prison, Axel's men hustle, as if they are heading to break up a brawl. A guard getting some snacks from the snack machine is alerted. He draws his gun, while curious inmates eavesdrop.

"Follow us, the alarm malfunctioned. There's a fight outside cells ten through fifteen," warns Ian Baynes.

The Guard remarks, "Trouble zone since fourteen went to the pit. Let's move it!"

They're now right in front of cell #15.

Ian Baynes grabs the prison guard around his neck. The Guard spins around facing Ian Baynes and Ricardo as his weapon falls to the ground. Two guns with silencers attached are pointing at him.

"Your clothes…and open fifteen! "

Commands Ian Baynes.

The Guard is bewildered until Ian Baynes quickly points the gun in his face. The Guard nervously disrobes, removes a bunch of keys from his belt, and unlocks the cell door.

Ian Baynes caps the Guard in the head, tosses his clothes to Ricardo, who hands them to Axel. Axel emerges from his cell, clothed in prison guard's uniform.

Ian Baynes and Ricardo drag the semi-nude guard inside cell # 15 and shut the door. They exit the prison interior, accompanied by Axel James.

The on-duty guard approaches the three of them questioningly.

"What is going on…with you three?"

"Going to get a smoke. We soon come back, yo hear?" Baynes, answers in patois and hands the Guard, a bag of weed. The three Drug Lords exit through the prison gates.

Outside the prison, Axel, Ian, and Ricardo get inside the black sedan and drive away, laughing hilariously.

10

BACK AT THE VILLA, A Jamaican Police Officer, armed like a SWAT member, ambulates outside the police cruiser. The Black sedan drives up, carrying the three Drug Lords. Axel barges out, followed by Ian and Ricardo. They immediately open silent fire on the police officer. His exchange is too late. Hit by several rounds, he falls to the ground while his ammunition soars. Axel pumps bullets into all four tires of his vehicle as well as the parked DEA Agent's car. Their black Sedan rolls up in the driveway. They are still oblivious of the search going on inside by the DEA.

Inside, Rude Buay and Hudson are now joined by Agent Scott, who recently aborted his surveillance duty on the exterior of the Villa. He rejoins his colleagues, with thumbs up, and assists in the assembling of the seizure, inside the living room.

A ray of light, reflects, shining into the living room, from the sedan's headlights.

The agents, sensing pending trouble, disperse respectively.

Scott leans up behind the front door.

Rude Buay goes through the back door, while Hudson hides behind the door to the first bedroom.

Axel James, now out of the car, reacts to the moving shadow behind the door of the first bedroom.

Axel James hints at Ian and Ricardo.

"We've got more company. PIGS! (Police) "

Rude Buay, not only notices Axel but hears his voice and adjusts for the perfect aim. He would rather take out Axel, but as soon as he gets the perfect aim on him, Axel darts in through the front door.

Already engaged, the bullet from Rude Buay's gun flies towards the sedan blows out its front windscreen. Ian Baynes and Ricardo, hiding on the ground, behind the back of the car, return gunfire, which misses Rude Buay, who dodges on time.

Behind the front door, Agent Scott and Axel James, end up in each other's space.

Scott tries to get a close-quarter shot off, but Axel "gets a drop" and the two engage in hand to hand combat. Axel out does Scott by a long shot.

Hudson emerges from behind the door and into the corridor. At the same time, Ricardo shotguns through the front door. Hudson, witnessing duel between Axel and Agent Scott gets an aim at Axel James' head. She shoots at Axel, simultaneously Scott punches Axel in the right eye; Axel rolls over. The bullet penetrates the wall.

Bullets go flying everywhere from Ricardo's gun like popcorn.

Before agent Hudson can retaliate, a bullet from Ricardo's gun grazes by her face. She's all shook up. Axel regains his presence of mind and lands a punch into Scott's stomach. Scott catches his breath.

Axel stumbles around with blurry vision.

On the outside of the Villa, Rude Buay, engages in a shootout with Ian Baynes. Both men miss their target. Finally, Ian reacts to being hit. He goes down. Rude Buay, satisfied, dashes to the inside through the front door.

Ricardo peripherally sees Rude Buay entering the house, and dashes towards the back door.

Ricardo, whispers to Axel,

"Let's get out of here, Boss."

Axel manages to recoup. They sprint to their car on the outside.

Ian Baynes, crawls in the back seat, with blood trickling down his neck.

Ricardo takes the wheel.

Axel scoots in on the other side.

The black car, with no front windshield, takes off in reverse, down the long, extended driveway.

Rude Buay, seeing the car disappear, rushes back outside, in frustration.

The black cat saunters across the driveway. Rude Buay aims at the animal but changes his mind.

Heavy pouring rain presents a hazard for Axel James, Ian Baynes, and Ricardo Herrera. They are not only soaking wet, but the car begins to swerve off the road. The sedan pulls over to the side of the road.

They exit. An approaching vehicle casts its light in their direction. The oncoming Mini-Van gets closer. The three men run out into the middle of the street. Their guns are drawn on the driver.

The Mini Van comes to a screeching halt, running off the road and into the gutter.

The Driver is a Rastafarian. Before he could get a word out, Axel James, shouts at him,

"Get out!"

The Driver complies and starts running for his life. Before he could escape, Axel pumps several bullets into his body.

The driver falls over the embankment. Axel follows him and confiscates his wallet.

They speedily transfer their cargo from the sedan to Mini Van, using it as their get-away vehicle.

The Mini Van pulls up outside the dock. A sailor from "The Tempest" waves in acknowledgment.

Axel James, Ian Baynes, and Ricardo step out and hurry on aboard the waiting yacht, with huge duffel bags.

The sailor lifts the yacht's anchor, while another releases the line and leaps back onto the sailing yacht.

At the Villa, sunrise casts its rays, as the three DEA agents vacate the premises.

They look at their sedan with its deflated tires.

Scott, the first one to speak, says:

"They could have already fled to Cuba."

Heidi Hudson, responds,

"With all that rain last night, driving without a front windscreen is impossible."

Rude Buay, after radioing for help, reminds them,

"I wouldn't put it past them. For all, you know they could have driven in reverse."

"Reverse? In the rain? On these winding roads? Asks agent Hudson.

"Yep! If the desire is strong enough, the facts carry no weight," replies, Rude Buay, as they wait next to the abandoned sedan.

11

TWO JAMAICAN POLICE Officers show up in an SUV and a land Rover. They jump out apologetically. The officer driving the jeep, hands over his keys to Rude Buay.

"You can use this," he instructs.

Rude Buay, looking at the jalopy, certainly does not resonate with it.

"Get us a helicopter, Officer," Rude Buay responds.

"That's not my call, Mr. Bascombe."

Rude Buay stares at him more intensely.

"Time is running out," remarks, Rude Buay, as he attempts to take the wheel of the SUV.

"Hold on, this is a Government Utility Vehicle. I am

the only one allowed to drive this GUV," says the other officer.

Rude Buay ignores him. The two other agents jump in. The officer retaliates. Rude Buay takes the wheel anyway, leaving both officers behind.

The retaliated officer, yelling in Patois, echoes,

"Don't you realize, the roads have changed! Motorists are skilled at driving in reverse. You need I and I to..."

Rude Buay, realizing, that he does need some help navigating, makes a roundabout turn. The officer hops in.

The *GUV* drives away followed by the Land Rover.

Later, a helicopter carrying Rude Buay, Scott and Hudson circles over the countryside. They spot an abandoned sedan on the roadside in Montego Bay. Moving in closer they discover the body of the car jacked Rastafarian in the gutter.

Scott, remarks, "Yep. These guys could have already fled the country."

"What if they're still here?" responds, Rude Buay.

Hudson, interjects.

"I doubt it,"

Rude Buay, unconvinced says,

"Navigating seems to be their cup of tea."

Hudson, using a pair of binoculars, notices as a tow-truck backs up to the Mini Van and engages in a tow. The name on the tow truck reads Black River Towing.

Later, the copter returns to the small Jamaican airstrip. Rude Buay and Scott step out. The accompanying officer directs Rude Buay and his agents to a parked sedan.

During this interim, cries from mourners are heard in the city of Mandeville, as more dead bodies are wheeled into a makeshift morgue. The stench is unbearable, coming from the regular, overcrowded facility next door.

Outside the hospital, hundreds of mourners congregate, waiting in tears to identify the body of their child.

"Could this have been prevented?" one mourner asks another.

"Yes, kids ought to learn not to play with matches," the intercepting Peace Keeping Officer responds.

The agents pull up outside Black River Towing.

Inside Rude Buay's car, his Pen Phone rings. He reviews the caller's ID. By the customary look on his face, his fellow agents suspect that it's their boss on the other end. So they eavesdrop.

"Hello. Agent Mendez," Rude Buay responds.

"Bascombe, we've been monitoring the Jamaican situation. Axel James and his allies have fled the country. Possibly to Cuba:" Jose Mendez remarks.

"Apparent, how? Is Castro signed on?" asks Rude Buay.

"What goes on in Cuba, stays in Cuba. My hands are tied. I'm having all three of you brought back to Miami tomorrow:" Mendez insists.

Rude Buay, says to Hudson and Scott, "Search has

been called off" and to Mendez, "We'll see you then."

12

IN A DOWNTOWN, ritzy, Miami hotel: Carlos, of
Asian descent, in his mid-thirties, removes his blood-
stained clothes and discards them in a black trash bag.
Semi-clothed, he rummages through a bag, scanning
through logs and other prison-related documents. He
goes to a suitcase, where he retrieves a toupee, and
carefully affixes it to his mask. He then removes four
Warden Uniforms from a suitcase and puts them on.
The name on his lapel reads Warden Richard Culligan.
Carlos takes a detailed look at himself in the full-length
mirror. Again, he studies Warden Culligan's picture,
scotch-taped to the wall next to the mirror. He uses
some paper tissue and creates padding for his biceps.
He is satisfied with his new look. Carlos picks up a
laden black duffel bag and departs.

A sedan pulls up outside Florida State Prison. Carlos steps out. He passes a prison guard, filing away paperwork in the booth.

"Wide-eyed and bushy-tailed?" Carlos, greets him, signing in.

"Hi Boss! Warden Culligan," replies the Guard.

"Anything to report, Miles?" Carlos asks.

The Guard responds,

"Everything's dandy, except that my replacement is usually here fifteen minutes early and he's..."

Carlos interrupts.

"I'll look into that for you."

Carlos proceeds towards Warden Culligan's office. He unlocks the door and enters. Shedding, three layers of prison uniform, Carlos deposits them; one per paper sack.

Outside Culligan's office, Bruce, the guard on patrol, ambulates. He removes a pack of cigarettes from his pocket, it's his last one. He lights up. Carlos steps out of the office, noticing Bruce's name tag.

Carlos, greets, "Hey Bruce, you got a cigarette?"

"Sorry, I've just smoked my last." Bruce responds.

"What you smoke, Salem?" asks Carlos.

Bruce nods, yes.

"You want to pick up a pack of Salem Lights?" asks Carlos.

"Yes Mr. Culligan," Replies Bruce.

He hands Bruce the money. Bruce departs.

Carlos makes his move, stopping in front of cell numbers one, twelve and thirty.

In cell # 1 resides Agnes Richards.

Carlos unlocks Agnes' cell and deposits a laden paper shopping bag. He hands Shelly a cellular phone along with a handwritten page of instructions. He departs.

In cell # 12 resides Denise Gomez.

Carlos unlocks Denise's cell and deposits a laden paper shopping bag. He hands her a cellular phone along with a handwritten page of instructions. He departs.

In cell # 30 resides Shelly Hall.

Carlos unlocks her cell and deposits a laden paper shopping bag. He hands Shelly a cellular phone along with a handwritten page of instructions. He leaves, noticed by other inmates and exits hurriedly. Most seem not to care. However, the Prison Guard at the booth, is somewhat confused, by all this unusual business.

"Warden Culligan, it's your off night. You're ..." he asks, inquiringly.

Carlos steps up closer to the booth and interrupts.

"Inside here your off night is always an on night. After your third month, you'll see what I mean."

The Prison Guard removes the sign-in sheet from the clipboard and sticks it in a brown manila envelope, sealing it with his saliva, then with scotch tape.

Carlos sensing the Prison Guards' strategic move to log a genuine report, eyes the clock inside the booth. The clock shows seven minutes to midnight. Carlos pushes the door open.

"So you're covering for him?" Carlos asks, and pulls out a semi-automatic from the duffel bag, with a silencer attached. He aims it at the guard.

Surprised, the guard remarks,

"You don't want to do that! I'll keep everything confidential. I swear..."

Carlos pumps several bullets into the Prison Guard's body. He falls outside of the booth, to the ground, to his death. Carlos PICKS up the handheld radio and radios. Three guards sitting in separate towers tune in. Carlos, announces:

"The next shift will be coming in five minutes early."

The Guards, respond,

"Good deal!"

Carlos picks up his cellular phone, and speedily, dials. Shelly, dressed in prison guard's attire, holding Automatic with a silencer attached and emerging from within prison compounds, answers.

"We are coming out!"

Shelly is oblivious, and steps on a line in the pavement. Immediately, the prison grounds floodlights come on all over the compound. The three women, attired in the Warden's uniform, disperse. They rush towards an individual, separate towers.

Now situated, they proceed to trade place with the three on-duty guards.

The guards, before completing their decent are shot simultaneously. They fall precipitously to their death.

The women race to the prison exterior, dash towards the sedan and enter like greased lightning. Carlos drives away.

Back at the State Prison, Bruce returns with the cigarettes but notices three empty cells as well as Warden Culligan's empty office. He's dumbfounded and confused.

Inside the car, Shelly, Agnes, and Denise rid themselves of the Warden's garb, revealing their true identity.

Suddenly the reflection of red and blue flashing lights stream inside the sedan. Sirens accompany the kaleidoscopic illumination.

Shelly, Agnes, and Denise reach for their gun simultaneously, in readiness.

The Miami police cruiser aggressively tails the sedan. The Sedan reduces its speed and moves to the right shoulder of the road. The Police cruiser stops closely behind. The Officer barges out, proceeds towards the driver's side of the sedan, and draws his gun.

Inside, the women, with guns still drawn, are poised, ready to shoot.

The officer proceeds with caution, trying to look through the rear tinted windscreen.

Instantly, three sets of bullets storm through the rear windscreen, laying the Officer flat onto the street.

The women return guns to the original position. Broken glass everywhere creates discomfort. The sedan speeds away and merges with the flow of traffic.

Moments later it drives into an underground parking lot where the limo waits.

Shelly, Agnes, and Denise exit. Still armed, they survey before getting inside the limo. The limousine door closes. It speeds off and merges into the flow of traffic, and subsequently arrives at the dock.

Carlos, Shelly, Denise, and Agnes join Alberto, already aboard his yacht, "Gomez".

Inside the other yacht, "Tempest," the phone rings. Axel, on deck, picks up.

"Axel, let's go to plan B." commands Alberto.

Axel reaches for and reviews the city of Port Antonio. He glances at his watch and responds.

"Okay, Boss! All the lights are green. Port Antonio by midnight."

13

THE "TEMPEST" SAILS BY Port Antonio's Peninsula. Axel James, Ian Baynes, and Ricardo dressed in wet suits, plunge into the water. Each carries a bag strapped to their back. The ship continues sailing towards Port Antonio, where it docks. A customs official boards the vessel. He inspects thoroughly. The captain of the Tempest over accommodates. Content the customs official returns to his booth.

In the wooded area of Port Antonio, shrubbery provides privacy, as Axel James, Ian Baynes, and Ricardo remove their water suits, dry off and get into street clothes retrieved from waterproof bags. They remove and open their duffel bags. Retrieving their weapons, they rush through the bushes.

They hit the streets of Port Antonio. A minivan designed to seat twelve passengers pulls up at the bus stop. They jump in. The door closes and it drives off.

The van, almost full to the max, with seats aligned theatre style and very little leg room between them, takes on the treacherous hillsides.

Ian Baynes, after finding a seat, takes out a wad of mixed currency and pays the conductor upfront. The locals, noticing the U.S. currency, eye him enviously. One man even sticks his hand out. Ian ignores the beggar's plea.

The Van stops. Axel James, Ian Baynes, and Ricardo exit and board another van.

This Van is filled mostly with Rastafarians wearing massive dreadlocks. The driver's dreadlocks are wrapped up in a knitted tam, black, yellow and green. Axel James studies the passengers, but mainly, two high school kids with untied shoe strings grab his attention.

Ian, eyes the driver, an Afro Asian.

"Central Port Antonio?"

"We just passed it!" replies the driver.

"Really?" asks Ian.

"Yes *mon*!" assures, the driver.

The Van stops. They get off.

Ian and Ricardo travel back on foot towards Avis and rent a white van. Axel and Ricardo await Ian's arrival. Ian pulls up in a white van. Axel and Ricardo jump aboard, duffel bags in hand.

Inside the Van, Axel unzips a duffel bag and admires his gun extensively. Finally, he utters,

"When do we return this vehicle?"

Ian, turning up the music, responds,

"All we have to do is call them at Avis if we need an extension. My brethren rule that joint, and besides…"

Axel James interrupts Ian,

"Where's your weapon?"

"My bag's behind the back seat. Where's base camp?" He answers.

Ricardo, interjects,

"Hope Bay! Close enough."

Ian replies, very sarcastically,

"Is that close to agent Banks?"

Ricardo eyes Axel questioningly.

Ian continues,

"Don't worry. We'll find Banks. First, we'll take out the government."

Axel, comments.

"Banks? He's small fry. If we could get the MP on our side…They wouldn't have a problem giving us the 411 on a former MP."

14

A SMALL DIMLY LIT HOUSE overlooks the city of Port Antonio. Lights from ships in the harbor create a picturesque subterranean backdrop.

Inside, maps, radios, headsets, binoculars, micro-cassette players and miscellaneous gadgets contribute to the ambiance. Walter Banks, an African American in his late fifties, with salt and pepper hair, sweats. He is fiddling disparately with his spy tech gadgets. An intermittent sound from his Pen Phone gets his attention. Banks retrieves it from his desk and listens in. The sound comes in and out, muffled; finally, he loses it.

On top of a mountain in Columbia, camouflaged between some trees, nestles a tiny shack built from wood and painted grass green. Chelo, a Colombian, dressed in a straw hat, ruffled clothing, and shoe-less, runs out of the shack. He tiptoes and adjusts the dismantled wire antenna on the roof. Like a champion, he hurries back inside.

The computer screen reveals a parked airplane at a Bogota location with a huge vacant cargo area. Scanning further, he notices several crates loaded with sacks of Dragon X Cocaine, destined for Port Antonio, Jamaica. He's possessed, like a kid in a candy store. The way he handles the mouse device, says he is hungry for this information. His screen reveals and captures an airport bus, registered to Bogota. Inside the bus, twelve teens take time to review instructions and small packets.

Walter Banks, sitting in his living room in Port Antonio, Jamaica, is enjoying the live feed. Suddenly, the computer screen goes blank. Banks desperately adjusts the picture via Tivo. He tunes in and replays.

Over the blank computer screen, he hears Chelo's voice.

"Come in Banks!"

"Go ahead Chelo." Banks replies.

Chelo, exclaims, "A huge shipment of contaminated Cocaine is being prepared. Destination, Port Antonio - Jamaica. The Dragon Drug Cartel has got it all lined up."

Banks, sharing Chelo's hunger for the info, reviews the

entire video.

Jumping up from behind his desk, he echoes,

"Bastards! Never!"

Banks goes to the window, pen phone in hand, taking in the harbor view. Nothing is visibly unusual, so he returns to his desk. Using the pen phone he writes on a slip of paper. He sticks the paper in an envelope and seals it with his saliva. Then he grabs his keys, along with the envelope and his Pen Phone.

He dashes outside to his car, turns it on and drives away.

An hour later, he arrives at the Ministry of Tourism and Culture Office in Kingston.

A red-eyed, Jamaican security guard, patrols the premises. Banks turns off the headlights. He travels on foot, eludes the guard and slips an envelope under the door, before exiting.

15

THE FOLLOWING MORNING, inside the Ministerial Building across the street, a meeting's in session. Five men dressed in suits, sit, facing each other, around a huge mahogany table.

Dalton Castello, the deputy Prime Minister, who is African American in his late forties, presides.

Michael Young, Caucasian, is in his early forties.

Vince La Borde, a bald African American, is in his mid-fifties. Bazil Taylor, African American, also is in his mid-fifties. William Russell, an African American, with salt and peppered hair.

This quintet of think tanks waits anxiously, ready to write.

Dalton Castello, addresses:

"The Prime Minister has asked me to preside over this meeting."

He searches through a stack of documents and continues.

"As you know he returns from CARICOM next week. The Jamaican economy is..."

The door opens. A drop-dead gorgeous, sophisticated, Mildred Simms, the desire of any man's heart, in her late twenties, enter.

Five pairs of eyes pierced her soul, questioningly.

Mildred, though slightly embarrassed for interrupting, radiates, "Excuse me!."

She hands the envelope to Dalton Castello and exits hurriedly. Castello opens the envelope and reads its contents.

"Gentlemen, it seems as if a Colombian Drug Cartel "The Dragons" is about to infiltrate our country with a shipment of over $25M worth of "cyanide-laced" cocaine. Our shores will now need to be guarded twenty-four-seven. Starting with Mo Bay. He EYES the clock on the wall and continues reading.

"They're known for taking out governments, they did in Grenada a few years ago. Watch your backs. Let's reconvene tomorrow."

Unnerved, they shut their folders and exit speedily.

Outside, a Mini Van stops, abruptly. Axel, Ian, and Ricardo jump out, armed with automatic weapons. The men are masked, with their tattoos covered up. A

Minister of Parliament standing outside acknowledges Axel and walks briskly ahead of them. As soon as they catch to the MP, he hands Axel a piece of paper. It's a blueprint. Axel, "crash studies" document.

They enter RAMBO STYLE. Two guards are jovially conversing inside the lobby. The guards, called to action, attempt to un-holster their uncompetitive weapons. The unwarranted visitors, quickly tie up the guards and throw them inside a closet. Proceeding, they meet the government ministers coming down escorted by a Police Officer. Before he could draw his gun, Axel shoots him in the chest. The Government Officials, scared out of their wits, try reversing upstairs.

Axel, commands:

"All we need is your cooperation. Your choice, resistance or termination? Extinction?"

Dalton Castello stares at Axel James with surprise.

Axel continues:

"Just do as you're told. Place your hands on top of your heads."

The five Ministers comply.

Axel, commandingly, directs:

"You are boarding the minivan across the street. Come on, move it!"

They are now on the outside, unnoticed, Ian Baynes opens the door to Mini Van.

Dalton Castello, Vince La Borde, Basil Taylor, Michael Young, and William Russell are forced inside. The

Mini Van speeds away.

16

INSIDE THE COMMISSIONER'S office, sits Commissioner Richard Baptiste, a tall, slim, kingly man in his forties. Sitting across from him is the governor-general Dr. Bradford Wiley, intellectually sound and in his sixties.

"We have no choice but to bring in **Rude Buay**," suggests, the commission.

Bradford Wiley, agitatedly, responds.

"Might as well sell our souls to the Devil."

"People like Rude Buay, get hired to find the Devil. Plus he has a vendetta - his brother. Make it happen...no matter what the cost," Advises the Commissioner.

The governor reminisces:

"We're still in a deficit from the last time, commissioner. Why should we have to pay for him? He's the son of our soil. JFK said, "Ask not what your country can do for you - ask what you can do for your country."

Richard Baptiste, explodes,

"This is Jamaica in crisis! The death toll has reached 150."

Bradford Wiley, shaken up and prayerfully composed, responds:

"Calm down Richard. Ask, and it shall be given you; seek, and ye shall find; knock, and it shall be opened unto you:

Matthew 7:7"

The Commissioner picks up his phone and dials.

At DEA Headquarters in Miami, the stone-faced Jose Mendez walks into the ringing of his office phone. He picks it up after the first ring.

"Jose Mendez!"

The Commissioner, responds,

"Mr. Mendez, this is Richard Baptiste the commissioner of police in Jamaica. As you know we've inherited Axel James and his allies from the U.S., as well as a huge epidemic; our kids are dying by the minute. We don't want to run our government using interns. Plus we're still recovering from the effects of that devastating hurricane. We need to broker a deal for Rude Buay's services.

Mendez replies,

"He's already headed back to Miami, and let me be clear...Rude Buay is the United States Drug Enforcement Agent, not a mercenary."

Baptiste, reminds him.

"You didn't have a problem taking a fee when his services were required prior..."

Mendez, matter-of-factly.

"Twenty percent increase and wire my handling fee to the same account as before. Happy hunting, Commissioner."

The Governor-General and The Commissioner shake hands and depart, accomplished.

17

A TAXI PULLS UP OUTSIDE the Michael Manley Airport departure terminal. Rude Buay, steps out followed by agent Hudson and Agent Scott. Rude Buay's cell phone rings. He answers.

"Bascombe, you've just been hired to put out Axel James' trash in Jamaica. It's a sizable raise from your last trip off of the reservation," commands, Jose Mendez.

Rude Buay, responds,

"According to Benjamin Disraeli: 'Nothing can resist the human will that will stake even its existence on its stated purpose."

Mendez, instructional replies,

"The Commissioner has already made arrangements for you and the team to meet him tomorrow in Montego Bay."

"There could be a conflict in the schedule as Mr. Banks is also expecting to meet with me tomorrow in Port Antonio."

Instructs, Rude Buay.

Jose Mendez responds sarcastically,

"What could a former MP do for you? That old racehorse is tired."

Rude Buay, disagreeing, remarks.

"The greatest tragedy in America is not the destruction of our natural resources, though that tragedy is great. The truly great tragedy is the destruction of our human resources by our failure to fully utilize our abilities, which means that most men and women go to their graves with their music still in them.' So said Oliver Wendell Holmes."

Hours later, the plane touches down at Montego Bay Airport. Rude Buay, Agent Scott, and Hudson deplane. Jamaican police patrol the grounds, armed with automatic weapons forming an impediment.

Mildred Simms is sandwiched like a rose between two sharp thorns, the commissioner to her left, Banks to her right.

Rude Buay emerges, followed by the agents. The commissioner greets.

"Welcome. Meet Mildred Simms, the eyes, and Banks, the ears, of Jamaica."

Rude Buay, replies,

"Meet my partners Agent Scott and Agent Hudson, if it moves he can drive it. If it's there, she can find it."

Glancing at Banks, he remarks.

"Mr. Banks, thanks for readjusting your..."

The Commissioner intercepts,

"Welcome Agent Scott and Agent Hudson."

Banks, announces.

"Jamaica? One Love!"

They walk over toward a waiting black Hummer.

Mildred Simms, states,

"In less than an hour, you'll be briefed on the current situation involving Axel James."

Banks, suggestively,

"Tonight we'll be partying Jamaican Style at the Beach Resort in Montego Bay. Sam's Taxi Tours will pick you up.'

Hudson, echoes,

"I love this place!"

Rude Buay, replies,

"I'm here to work, Mr. Banks."

To which, Banks responds,

"You have to assimilate into your environment, no?"

Hudson, wastes no time, securing the seat belt around her. Rude Buay and Scott throw the luggage inside the Hummer, they climb in as the hummer departs.

In the meantime, at an Airfield in Port Antonio, a small aircraft touches down. Passengers of Colombian decent rush from the aircraft and onto a waiting bus.

The bus drives away.

Additionally, on top of an Ocho Rios hillside, Jamaican police comb through the bamboo trees with dogs in search of Axel, Ian, and Ricardo Hererra.

In a Mandeville park, a posted sign reads: PARK CLOSED UNTIL FURTHER NOTICE.

Outside a Vegetable Market, in Kingston,

Produce is off-loaded from trucks. Desperate shoppers bid for supply in quantity, fearing a scarcity.

At a tenement yard in Kingston, where Rude Buay once lived, a couple stack up on food supply of corned fish, starch, canned foods, rice, peas, flour, sugar, and cooking oil.

Over the airwaves, the breaking news continues. One announcer throws himself into it. He reports:

"Power 106 FM. Radio Jamaica on the go. Gas prices continue to soar. While several vehicles wait in line at the pumps. The Jamaican coast guard cutter aggressively patrols the shores. Helicopters fly at low altitudes to find Members of the Dragon Drug Cartel. Meanwhile, the death toll continues to climb as several adults have also lost their lives as a result of using contaminated drugs. Sources close to the Prime Minister's Office claim that American DEA agents are expected to be briefed shortly regarding this fiasco, as five Government officials are still missing."

On several drug trafficking streets in Port Antonio, MP's oversee the setup of roadblocks. In particular, those leading towards the airfield. Several locals wait in line with parked vehicles, as individuals displaying Dragon tattoos, exchange sacks of cocaine for cash.

18

OUTSIDE THE CROWDED Port Antonio Hospital E.R., many patients lay waiting on gurneys. Despite her medical garb, stunningly eye-catching, 25-year-old, Attending Physician, Dr. Tamara Ross, draws applause - mainly from the male gender. She is focused as she enthusiastically watches over the growing life and death drama of the ill-fated children.

In Kingston, outside the police barracks, the streets are lined with early morning vendors, flanged by carnival demonstrators. The Jamaican and U.S. flags wave in the breeze. Steve, in his 50s, shirtless, establishes the tune on his steel pan.

Steve, in a rugged falsetto, sings:

"Don't stop the carnival. Down with the criminals. We

want Steel band, Calypso, and Mardi Gras."

The black Hummer pulls up, sandwiched by Jamaican police on motorbikes. Rude Buay, Agent Scott, and Hudson step out and enter through the police barracks.

Jamaican policemen gait excessively. Seated behind a long desk are the Governor-General Dr. Bradford Wiley, Deputy Police Commissioner Winston Davis, and the honorable, Pete Bacchus. Seated in front of the desk are Prison Warden, Ralph Bullock, Mildred Simms, and five distinguished officers of the Jamaica police force. Rude Buay, Scott, and Hudson walk in, occupying the front row seats. Police Commissioner Richard Baptiste, emerges from the back room and sits next to the Governor-General. They shake hands. Jamaican police officers close the door. The Commissioner stands and addresses:

Good morning. I'd like to introduce, The Governor-General of Jamaica, Dr. Bradford Wiley.

Applause! The Commissioner sits.

Dr. Bradford Wiley stands up and removes an index card from his breast pocket. He puts on his reading glasses, and after glancing at the index card, addresses the working group.

"Rude Buay, Agent Scott, and Agent Hudson welcome to Jamaica."

He continues,

"Our collaborative efforts in finding the missing and

ensuring that justice is served will certainly protect the lives of our future generation: THE KIDS."

The gathering applauds.

Dr. Wiley removes his reading glasses, puts them inside the case, and sits down. The projector light comes on. Police Commissioner, Richard Baptiste stands. He points to the screen.

A picture of exhibit #1: Axel James.

Baptiste, continues,

"Axel James, mid-30s, Columbian decent, scarred, and stone-faced. Axel a fugitive, murderer, drug lord, sailor and con artist."

Next, a picture of exhibit #2: Ian Baynes

Baptiste, continuing:

"Ian Baynes, mid-30s, African American."

Followed by a picture of exhibit #3: Ricardo Herrera.

Baptiste states,

"Ricardo Herrera, early 40s, Colombian descent. Both are known associates of Axel James and equally have extensive rap sheets throughout the Islands and several of the Southern States. They are known also as gang members of the notorious Dragon Drug Cartel."

Next, a picture of exhibit #4: Dalton Castello.

There is silence, you can hear a pin drop.

The Commissioner, echoes,

"Dalton Castello, Minister of National Security (Police, Prisons, and Seaports)! The Public Service and Airport Development. Missing!"

A picture of exhibit #5: Michael Young, follows.

Baptiste, echoes,

"Michael Young, Minister of Tourism and Culture. Missing!"

A picture of exhibit #6: Vince La Borde, follows.

Baptiste, continues.

"Vince La Borde, Minister of Telecommunications, Science Technology and Industry. Social Development, the Family, Gender and Ecclesiastical Affairs. Missing!"

A picture of exhibit #7: Bazil Taylor, appears.

Baptiste continues.

"Bazil Taylor, Minister of Transport, Works and Housing. Missing."

Followed by, a picture of exhibit #8: William Russell

He continues,

"William Russell, Minister of State in the Ministry of Education, Youth and Sports. Missing!

The projector light goes off.

The Commissioner engages the podium. All eyes are focused on him as he expounds:

"Those ministers of government were kidnapped at the Economic debate... The carnival celebrations are still on hold for security reasons. Agents, your assistance in this crisis is invaluable."

He shakes hands with the Minister of Health and Environment, Honorable Esther Graves. Then he exits briskly on heels of the Governor-General.

Rude Buay, stares at prison Warden Ralph Bullock, a man of East Indian descent, with displeasure. His name tags glitter in the dimly lit room of aggravated government officials.

Mildred Simms moseys out from the briefing room, and connects with Rude Buay.

"Rude Buay, the Governor-General wants to see you in his office."

Rude Buay leaves Bullock an eye full of "it's all good." Inside the Conference Room, the Governor-General and Commissioner sit face to face.

Mildred Simms enters, followed by Rude Buay.

Wiley greets them and remarks,

"Rude Buay, whatever you need. The Commissioner and his team are here for you."

Rude Buay, without batting an eye, replies,

"I need maps containing every street, track, river, stream, gutter, sewage line, mountain, hill and valley, blueprints of buildings, homes, huts, outhouses, and every dog house and "pig pen" in Port Antonio. Plus, I need Helicopters, speedboats and fast automobiles."

He pauses, and then continues:

"If a hammer hits a nail on its head there after today I want to know who did it and where."

The Commissioner responds,

"Why our police barracks?"

"Because you never know who is rolling in the **mud**."

The Commissioner, eyes Wiley and Mildred, then focuses on Rude Buay.

"And how soon do you need these?"

Rude Buay, responds,

"Tomorrow by sunset."

Mildred Simms looks at the Governor-General.

Baptiste eyes Rude Buay with concern.

Wiley ponders before responding.

"Rude Buay, we don't have enough manpower. We have access to one extra helicopter, which we borrow from Haiti only on Sundays…Two coast guard cutters and they've been working around the clock, since…We have one Hummer, the next shipment has been delayed…"

Rude Buay, says to Scott,

"Get on the phone. We have a few favors to call in. Ask Banks to show up half an hour earlier."

Scott, questioningly,

"Am I in this meeting?"

Rude Buay, responds, sarcastically,

"Only if you speak Patois."

Rude Buay shake hands with Baptiste and Wiley. Mildred Simms escorts him to the door. She waves goodbye.

Mildred returns to the room. The Commissioner walks over to Mildred and addresses her in Patois.

"Keep a close eye on Mr. Rude Buay and his partners. Don't lose them out of your sight. This isn't his show. He's our… "

Mildred senses his trend of thought and trails Rude
Buay.

19

SAM'S TAXI TOUR bus arrives at the dock in Negril. Rude Buay, Agent Scott and Hudson step out dressed to the nines.

A short Jamaican Police patrolling, carrying semi-automatics, approach the agents. Five additional officers, observe.

The officer confronts the agents.

"May I take a look at your ID's?" he asks.

Like clockwork, the three DEA agents flash their badges.

Police continue,

"I'm sorry, but you're not allowed."

Rude Buay, replies,

"Looks like you boys didn't get the memo."

The Police replies,

"What "memo" would that be, Mr. American tourist?"

Rude Buay, lashes out at him after that comment.

"The "memo" that this "tourist" is here to save your country from the bad guys."

The other five policemen advance. Six weapons are now pointed at Rude Buay, but before they know it, Rude Buay, Scott and Hudson have swiftly disarmed and subdued two of them. The remaining Police train their weapons on the two Agents. Five additional police officers draw closer towards the agents with guns cocked.

There's radio transmission. The Policemen, listen in.

Mildred's voice echoes,

"Send Rude Buay and Scott and Hudson in. Over."

Rude Buay and Scott release their captives and are promptly escorted inside.

An Elderly man yells from the crowd in Patois.

"Yardy Buay come home to roost with Yankee gal!"

Rude Buay ignores the welcome.

A Police Officer escorts them inside Negril Beach Hotel.

Mildred is sitting alone at a table.

Rude Buay rambles in her direction, with agent Scott and Hudson tailing him. Banks is at the bar drinking a beer. Rude Buay, pulls up a stool next to Banks.

"Pardon my tardiness. What can I say about some of these locals?"

Remarks, Rude Buay.

"They see you as a sophisticated American, who has a vendetta against them. But it's all good. Now, how can I help you?"

Says, Banks,

Rude Buay, takes a beer and responds.

"Your commissioner wants me on this case but their resources are so limited."

Banks' very diplomatic. Ponders, then states,

"I still have some Cuban ties."

Mildred gets up from her seat at the table and walks over to the bar.

"Mr. Rude Buay. Your agents are waiting for Sir," States Mildred.

"Let's talk later, Mr. Banks,"

Says, Rude Buay, excusing himself.

Rude Buay, joins the others at the table.

Mildred, observing him closely, states,

"Welcome to NEGRIL Resort."

Maitre D steps up and seats them and leaves.

Agent Scott scans the room discreetly. The dance floor is crowded. Booze is everywhere. The DJ plays a slow song.

Rude Buay and Mildred exchange glances.

Hudson, jealously, clues in.

Mildred continues,

'Would you like to dance Rude Buay?"

Mildred Simms gets up and leads Rude Buay to the dance floor.

Scott notices a hot woman sitting alone at another table. She winks at him, and touches her neck, on the jugular vein. Scott clues in, that's how the women in that clique introduce themselves. Scott strolls in her direction. Her added smile says to Scott, "we belong." Scott leads her to the dance floor. Hudson is left alone at the table.

Hudson scouts, looking for someone she could lead to the dance floor. She notices Scott, as he departs with the woman.

Shelly, Agnes, and Denise, all wearing bandanas, arrive at the dock. They huddle with Jamaican police officers. The Officers point them in the direction of the resort.

Inside, Rude Buay and Mildred pass by the bar, en route to a busy dance floor.

Banks, full of man talk, cautions.

"Easy now, Rude Buay!"

Rude Buay smiles.

Banks resumes,

"Enjoy the music "Reggae Style."

The Bartender serves Banks another beer. A Local joins Banks with "cheers".

Banks asks the local,

"Are you participating in the festivities?"

The Local, responds.

"Not this year, Banks."

Banks, follows up.

"Burnt out?"

The Local replies,

"Drug lords are seeking refuge here. On top of that, cops get shot down like flies and five government officials... Who wants to venture out and get shot?"

Banks looks at his beer, takes a calculated sip.

Banks encapsulates,

"It used to be Jamaica "One Love" until..."

Rude Buay and Mildred Simms return to the table. Banks' eyes are fixed on them, wishing it was him in pursuit of the Jamaican beauty, Mildred.

Banks turns to leave.

"So, tomorrow we'll continue our manhunt?"

States, Rude Buay.

Banks returns to the bar.

Mildred addresses Rude Buay.

"Yep. You find Axel first or I will."

The Waiter brings another round of drinks. Mildred removes the cherry from her drink and dangles it in front of Rude Buay's face. Finally, she puts it inside her mouth and chews the life out of it.

Rude Buay feels like Mildred has thrown a ninety mile an hour curveball.

Adjusting, he asks,

"How much does Banks know?"

Mildred, responds.

"His grey hair speaks for itself, Mr. Rude Buay."

Rude Buay, remarks.

"You've called me that name twice tonight. Are we

going to be able to keep this on a business level?"

To which, she responds,

"All I can say is, 'what is to be will be.' Sir."

Rude Buay excuses himself from the table and moves into Banks' space. Mildred pursues. Hudson remains at the table writing in her journal. She sees the three all familiar women. Before she could respond in self-defense, they offensively, have invaded her space.

Shelly whacks Hudson in the head with her automatic weapon. Hudson falls to the ground and struggles to get up. Shelly whacks her again. This time, she falls to the ground hard. Denise grabs her, blindfolds her, and escorts her through the back entrance.

BANG, BANG, BANG. GUNSHOTS.

People run for cover. Beer bottles, from aroused locals, are hurled in direction of the bar, accompanied by gunshots from the three women. Rude Buay and Scott, struck by beer bottles, hit the floor. Getting up they give chase, trying to get an aim in through the dense crowd.

Agnes sticks a rag inside Agent Hudson's mouth, seals it with duct tape, and quickly binds her with rope.

There's a huge crowd of people trying to get out. Agent Scott exits through the side doors.

Mildred Simms follows close behind.

Banks notices an unclaimed lady's purse on Mildred's table. Next to it lies a napkin, drawn on it, in red ink, a dragon.

He yells,

"Miss Simms, you forgot something."

Mildred turns around, goes back to retrieve it. She notices the Dragon tattoo drawn on the napkin. Mildred reflects. She had seen the same signature worn by agent Scott, earlier at the table.

Outside the resort, the three women rush Hudson aboard a speed boat.

Rude Buay pursues on foot. He runs into two Jamaican police officers. Rude Buay pushes his way through, slightly brushing against one of the officers who loses his balance in the process. Several Officers respond in retaliation.

Mildred rushes out and sedates Rude Buay. Meanwhile, the boat speeds off. Leaving Rude Buay along with white water waves at the vacant dock.

Agent Scott returns. Rude Buay notices. Not pleased about his absence during a manhunt of this magnitude addresses Scott.

" You missed it huh? Did she French kiss you on the brain?"

Agent Scott claims,

"Too many double-crossers."

Rude Buay responds,

"Welcome to the real WAR, Manhunt in the Caribbean"

20

INSIDE THE NEGRIL HOTEL, Rude Buay, sits at a desk conducting a database search of names on the computer. His Pen Phone rings. The caller ID reveals Mendez's number.

Rude Buay takes the call.

"This is no good. Bascombe, what did you find out on Hudson?" remarks Mendez.

Rude Buay responds,

"Nothing so far."

Mendez replies,

"Rude Buay, it's clear that you failed to cover her."

Rude Buay, getting straight to the point, responds.

"Hold on! Are you accusing me of... Chief, this had to have been a..."

Mendez questions,

'By who?"

Rude Buay, replies,

"I'm still gathering info. Possibly the three female fugitives."

Mendez responds,

"Are you trying to say that they escaped from prison in less than twenty-four hours and are already raining on your parade?"

Rude Buay states,

"They showed up in Jamaica. How did they know where to find her?"

Says Mendez,

"No idea! Bascombe, you've left me with only one choice... I'm going to have to bring you back to The U.S."

Rude Buay responds,

"Never! Why? So that the drug Lords feel that they've won? We're flirting with the possibility of having Hudson's body returned to us in a body bag. Never! I will never concede!"

Mendez continues to break him down.

"You begged to have her and agent Scott join you. We don't want to have their bodies returned to us in caskets."

Rude Buay states,

"I need time...as well as resources. Plus there are too many probabilities."

Mendez reminds him.

"We don't have much of it."

Rude Buay, cogitates, then responds.

"48 hours?"

Mendez replies,

"When and if you get into my seat, you can run things your way, but until then, in this department, what I say goes. This case is going to be... reassigned. Rude Buay, you begged for this assignment. Plus, her son calls you Uncle Rude Buay. You're not even..."

Rude Buay, senses not only the racist overtone but for the first time, his boss called him by his local name. Could his boss be in on this also? He ponders before responding.

"Too many cooks spoil the broth."

Jose Mendez persisting,

"That's all you have 47 hours 59.30 minutes."

Rude Buay replies.

"I'll take you up on that mandate, but from here on in, I am going to run things my way. This is my soil."

21

INSIDE THE HOTEL ROOM, Rude Buay engages in a set of pushups. His hotel phone rings. The thought occurs. Could this be his boss? He grabs it.

"Rude Buay, this is Alberto. I can tell you that you are not a good swimmer. Anyway getting down to business, I have your partner. In exchange for her, I want you out of the Caribbean for good. For Good! In 24 hours I'll have a jet waiting to fly you back to Miami. My peeps will contact you."

"How much?" asks Rude Buay.

Alberto, responds,

"I don't need the cash. I just want you out of Jamaica."

Rude Buay, replies:

"This is the land of my birth. I will not give up this

right to... I will fight in the hills, in the valleys, on the seas, in the air, underground. If I go down I will go down fighting!"

Alberto, responds.

"A very poor rendition of Winston Churchill..."

Rude Buay, hangs up the phone and researches on his computer. The name Alberto Gomez surfaces. He double clicks on the profile. An error message comes up: INFORMATION NOT AVAILABLE. He inputs the name for a second time. Same result. Rude Buay picks up the phone and dials.

On Walter Banks' wall, there's a portrait of Banks and Chelo. The red phone, sitting on his desk keeps ringing. No body's there. Rude Buay dials a different number.

"You've reached 876-322-7171. Leave a message after the beep."

He does not leave a message.

On the beach, Banks lies on the sand. He's cuddled up next to a hot babe sharing a beach towel. Waves wash up against their feet.

Rude Buay dials in desperation.

At the office of Tourism and Culture, Mildred Simms picks up the phone.

"This is Mildred Simms!"

"Mildred, this is Rude Buay. An assignment has been thrown at me. What do you know about...Alberto Gomez?" Waiting for her response, he gets ready to write.

Mildred responds:

"Nothing. I've never heard of him. Banks should have more of the inside scoop on him."

Rude Buay asks,

"Where's he?"

Mildred, licks her lips before responding.

"It's a sunny day, try the beach. He likes playing Casanova. It's the Island in him"

Rude Buay, asks.

"Which beach?"

Mildred responds.

"It's 96 degrees in the shade and the water stays warm all night long."

Rude Buay informs her.

"I've got a big fish to deep fry. If you hear from Banks, tell him to call me ASAP."

Mildred replies,

"It's apparent that you are going to have a fish frying party before this whole thing washes out. Huh??

Rude buay, responds, "Thanks. I need a 20 on Scott."

Mildred replies,

"To the best of my knowledge, he's with that woman from the party. They both display similar tattoos."

Rude Buay cautions.

"No one gets my whereabouts except Mr. Banks.

Rude Buay hangs up. "

Rude Buay's phone rings.

He picks up.

"This is Bascombe".

Banks, voice comes in.

"Rude Buay..."

Banks' on the phone.

Rude Buay enthusiastically,

"Walter Banks! The man of the hour. Banks, I know that you're a beach bum, but I've got something that might interest you. How would you like to team up with me?"

Banks asks,

"Why?"

Rude Buay responds.

"I've got a big fish to fry. The agency is trying to hold me responsible...for the kidnapping of Heidi Hudson. All I have to go on is a name... Alberto Gomez."

Banks, asks with concern:

"How do I come in?"

Rude Buay answers.

"I need a guy who knows them inside out. I understand that you've spent several years working underground in Bogota and an MP for the Jamaican government."

Banks replies,

"I let sleeping dogs lie."

Rude Buay states,

"I'll protect you exclusively."

Banks asks,

"What about your guys?"

Rude Buay replies.

"You know how shafted these guys are. I need
someone who can deliver. Someone with a destiny
and a passion and purpose to fulfill it.
Banks replies,
"I believe in priorities."
Rude Buay, interrupts.
"God, family, job..."
Banks interrupts,
"Country! You don't identify with us."
After a beat, Banks continues.
"It was Kennedy who said: Ask not what your
country can do for you - ask what you can do for your
country."
Rude Buay informs,
"So said your commissioner."
Rude Buay, reflects, then continues,
"Except that he forgot that: A man without vision
shall perish."
Banks, has had enough. He responds.
"Rude Buay I've been there, done that. Don't need
your third party tactics. How much?"
Rude Buay responds,
"Half a mil..."
Banks inquires,
"Who picks up the tab?"
Rude Buay assures,
The PEPI account.
"I'm in."

Says Banks.

Banks hangs up the phone and immediately surveys the coastline using his binoculars. He reaches into his pocket, retrieves his Pen Phone and dials and makes contact.

"Come in Chelo."

Chelo responds,

"Come in Banks."

Banks replies.

'Go ahead Chelo. What you got?"

Chelo, always excited when he discovers a plot:

"A blue ship operated by the dragon cartel bearing the name "Tempest" has dropped off a shipment last night in Mo Bay. It could be heading your way, pronto.

Banks responds,

"Thanks. I've got it on the radar as we speak. By the way, I need everything on Don Alberto Gomez."

Chelo, not sure.

"I don't know...Maybe..."

Banks demands,

"Everything!"

Banks hangs up and dials.

Rude Buay answers.

"Rude Buay, this is Banks. A blue ship named "Tempest" has stepped into our radar. Destination: Negril. Mildred will meet you onboard "Hairoun" at the Negril's Dock. The coast guard ship will be tailing you."

Rude Buay exuberantly,

"Good. Very good."

Rude Buay get up from his chair, STRAPS a gun to his left leg and summons agent Desmond Scott.

22

NEGRIL OVERLOOKS A VAST body of blue water, a variety of ships nesting on it. White sand beaches, hilltop houses, and trees provide a paradisiacal backdrop. Sounds of horns and engines from ships on the go drown out the sound of waves washing up against the shoreline. The water reflects the rays from the sun.

Rude Buay scans the harbor through binoculars. He zooms in for clarity. He spots the "Tempest." But notices that its country of origin is missing.

Rude Buay adjusts the focus and notices the transferring of cargo from yacht to yacht.

Mildred's hair blows in the wind. She looks through

her binoculars to catch that view..

Rude Buay says to Scott.

"Do you see what I see?"

Scott responds.

"No. Not really."

Rude Buay indicates,

"Straight ahead to the left."

Agent Scott fires up the engine.

Their ship Hairoun picks up speed, heading in direction of the suspected ship. It drops anchor. Rude Buay and Mildred climb aboard the Tempest.

Rude Buay and Mildred proceed with weapons drawn; they amble closer.

There's a shadow.

Rude Bauy, yells.

"Freeze! DEA."

The sailor hastily releases the anchor chain and dives into the water. Three men wearing masks emerge on deck, with guns drawn.

Rude Buay continues.

"Drop your weapons! Now! "

Ian Baynes comes out from the hull of the ship, wearing a blue expensive business suit and dark sunglasses. His gun is drawn.

Ian yells.

"You're trespassing! Private property."

Ian is distracted by two Jamaican and one Cuban coast guard, cutting water, heading in that direction. Three Jamaican coast guard officers and one Cuban aim towards the Tempest with a drawn semi-automatic.

It's now a standoff. The Jamaican coast guard officers concentrate their aim on the masked men. Meanwhile, a Haitian Helicopter circles overhead.

Rude Buay commands.

"Drop your weapons!"

They hesitate.

Rude Buay shoots. The bullet hits the "made-over" Ian Baynes in the chest. He falls overboard.

Scott remarks,

"Maybe he'll listen next time."

Coast guard officers dive into the water and fish out Ian, who happens to still be alive. They drag him aboard the coast guard boat. Blood is pumping out of bullet hole in his chest.

Jamaican Police place cuffs on the other three men: Michael Cox, Sebastian Perez, and Nigel Davis.

Rude Buay and Scott proceed into the hull of the ship, with Banks in tow. Mildred guards the deck. They cautiously enter.

Rude Buay stops abruptly, listen, and then moves a few steps, with ears cocked. He hears a squeaky sound. He draws up behind the door and opens it. The way looks clear so he beckons Scott in his direction.

Scott ambles up close to him. Banks follows in tow. There's another door. They try to open it but it's locked. The sign on it says: ENGINE ROOM DOOR MUST BE KEPT CLOSED.

Rude Buay glances back at Scott. Moves to the other side of the door and begins to grasp the handle. He checks his gun, grabs the doorknob, swings it open and charges in with Agent Scott and Banks on his tail. They scan the room hastily.

Rude Buay notices some canvas draped like a table cloth. He grabs it in disgust, throwing it on the floor. There's a lid. Rude Buay lifts it off.

INSIDE: Stacks of twenty-dollar bills in Jamaican currency, binoculars, hammocks, blankets, and survival kits and grenades and a huge gun collection. Another lid gets Rude Buay's attention.

Inside: Dalton Castello's body, bound with ropes, wounds to the head; he's still breathing. So they carry him up to the deck, to be transported to the hospital.

23

THE AMBULANCE PULLS UP in front of the E.R. entrance at Port Antonio Hospital. Medics wheel out a gurney with Castello on it. Simultaneously, a Taxi pulls up to the gate. Out steps, Tamara Ross, she's dressed in blue scrubs, a stethoscope hanging from her neck. She hustles through the entrance to the E.R. and assists in treating Mr. Castello.

A pot of coffee is brewing in the kitchen at Banks' house. Steelpan music is playing in the background. Rude Buay is admiring the view of the Port from the window. Banks returns with a huge roll of blueprints. Rude Buay, looking out the window, exclaims,

"Great View!"

Banks replies,

"Like a basin decorated with toy boats."

Rude Buay returns to the dining room table, now cluttered with blueprints.

Rude Buay follows up on his comment.

"Yep! Do you sail, Banks?"

Banks, enjoying the conversation:

"I love yachts."

Rude Buay feeds his ego.

"You must have captured some great pictures from this location."

Banks responds,

"Oh yes, but most of my pictures come from Bogota'.

Rude Buay asks,

"Great place?"

Banks, replies,

"I spent five years there, working undercover for the U.N."

"What was it like?"

Asks Rude Buay, with concern.

Banks replies,

"Scary. One moment you're alive knowing that the next moment you could be eaten by vultures flying overhead."

Banks shows him a stack of pictures. One has a man wearing the dragon tattoo. Rude Buay clues in.

Banks, continues.

"The night they caught Chelo taking pictures of their operation, they captured him and decided to hang him."

Rude Bauy, likes what he hears, plus, being able to build such a bridge with his new sidekick, is invaluable, so he asks.

"Really?"

Banks relays.

"I rode into their camp strapped to the chassis of the truck driven by the guy who was commissioned to hang Chelo. When the truck stopped, I untied myself and waited underneath. The Driver stepped out, I grabbed him by his feet, took him down, crawled out, grabbed his rifle, wasted him, put his clothes on, drove Chelo to the gallows site and shot the men waiting for "the Kill." Chelo and me been buddies ever since."

Rude Buay enquires further.

"How did you learn about their plan?"

Banks, full of wisdom, responds,

"When your ear's to the ground you learn many things, my friend."

Rude Buay, feeling as if he had just received some food for thought, responds,

"Tell me about Alberto Gomez."

Banks, opening up.

"Man's like a sealed case. He's not your average Czar."

Rude Buay inquires,

"Who funds him?"

Banks responds,

"Your agency hasn't...?"

Banks phone rings. He answers.

Chelo's voice is like music to his ears.

"Banks what I know you already know..."

Rude Buay eavesdrops.

Banks replies,

"Thanks!"

Banks realizes that there is nothing new on Alberto. So he continues informing Rude Buay.

"They claim that he has billions in Swiss accounts, yet nothing has turned up in his name. He posted record profits in the last two years. He controls most of the traffic up and down the coast. Axle James' former boss, he's married to Denise Gomez, whom you busted last year."

Rude Buay reminisces.

'No wonder she's broken out of prison so easily." He ponders, then continues his series of questions.

"Where does he reside?'

Banks replies,

"Every agent who has met with him in person is already dead or on his waiting list. His home address is never published. No landline telephone. His ships are not registered. He owes the IRS over $2.8 Million in back taxes. They can't bring him down. The man's untouchable."

Rude Buay, asks.

'How do we get him?"

"Make contact with his wife Denise; hold her as ransom. We could start there,"

Banks says.

Rude Buay questions.

'Could she be our doorway to Heidi Hudson?"
Banks remarks,
"They work independently at times but they could
have teamed up on kidnapping of this magnitude."
Rude Buay's cup is full.
"Where there's a will there's a way."
Banks says sarcastically,
"I thought that your Mom practiced..."
Rude Buay, with limited knowledge of the craft,
replies,
"She never taught me the tricks. Said it will make me
mentally lazy. Neither did she leave a catalog in her
WILL."
Banks, continuing like a runaway train, declares.
"When the Philistines wanted to take out Samson, they
went through Delilah."
Rude Buay ponders that gesture, then immediately
thereafter, picks up the pen phone and dials. He
receives a busy tone. Meanwhile, Banks phone rings in
the other room. Banks leaves to get it. Rude Buay re-
dials.
Rude Buay reaches Mildred.
"Mildred, I am having a challenge getting through to
the commissioner. He's not..."
Mildred replies,
"It's 2:00 a.m Rude Buay, I'll get him for you."

24

THE PHONE RINGS inside the Commissioner's bedroom. Commissioner Richard Baptiste and his wife Christine are asleep in bed. He snores like a freight train. She rolls over, pokes him in the ribs, then grabs the phone.

Mildred echoes.

"Richard! Richard!"

Christine responds.

'He's..."

Christine jealously looks at the clock, and continues.

"Mildred he's fast asleep after a steamy night. I'll tell him that you called. Is there a message?"

Mildred responds,

"Police business."

Christine is about to hang up.

Richard rolls over and tugs the receiver from her.

She removes the handcuffs from bed-head, opens the night stand's draw, deposits them, and meanders towards the bathroom - semi-clothed.

Richard, occupied with the phone call, says,

"Hello?"

Mildred responds,

"Commissioner, I have Rude Buay on a 3-Way call."

The Commissioner senses serious business by this 2:00 a.m. call.

Rude Buay informs,

"Commissioner, Rude Buay here. I didn't mean to wake you."

The Commissioner, still half asleep,

"Rude Buay, didn't you get them?..."

Rude Buay informs,

"If we, meaning, U.S. Government personnel and equipment were to guard the shores tomorrow, would you have enough manpower available to piggy-back our effort?"

Commissioner responds,

"That's a rather hypothetical question."

The Commissioner composes himself and continues.

"Why do we need to guard the shores?"

Rude Buay, wishing the Commissioner gets his concept, replies,

"It's a possible escape route that Axel James and his men could use. If he rejoins Alberto we could have more trouble on our hands. Agent Hudson could be history."

To which the Commissioner responds,

"Do you have any idea as to how much it's going to cost the government of Jamaica to carry out such a feat? On top of that our police force is already working over time."

Rude Buay goes for the jugular.

"Let me put it like this...for a few extra dollars, you can either help save your country from the tyranny of the Axel James' of the world or become pawns under the weight of their oppressive cartels?"

Commissioner Baptiste responds,

"We're already over budget on you Mr. Rude Buay. That Cuban helicopter drinks up a lot of fuel."

Christine returns all dolled up and crawls in bed.

The Commissioner continues,

"Plus, that's not the way we do things here."

"This is your baby. Plus you couldn't pay me if you wanted to." replies Rude Buay.

Baptiste looks over at Christine and says.

"I'll have a word in at sunrise,"

and hangs up.

25

RUDE BUAY, LOOKS across at Banks, who is head-bopping frequently. Rude Buay picks up his phone and dials.

At The DEA office in Miami, Mendez walks out towards the door, attaché case in hand. His phone rings. He returns to his desk. Picks up. Looking at the caller ID, he sees agent Bascombe's number displayed. "This better be good," he says under his breath.

Picking up, Rude Buay, addresses him.

"Mendez! Bascombe here."

Mendez expecting great news:

"Lay it on, Rude Buay!"

Rude Buay responds.

What are the chances of rescinding the offer?

Mendez replies.

"Which offer?"

Rude Buay reflects and feels like he's now in a vice. He wants to save his country, but trust is waning in these critical moments. His existing team of U.S. agents is down to the rather untrustworthy, Desmond Scott. His sidekick, Banks, wakes up and pours two cups of coffee. He hands one to Rude Buay.

Rude Buay, responds to Mendez's question.

"The one that you've made with the Commissioner."

Mendez looks at his Rolex. Admiring it, states,

"Why? What's the hurry Rude Buay?"

Rude Buay responds,

"Everyone seems to be in on this including the man who brokered the deal with you."

Mendez replies.

"Are you saying that you don't trust your countrymen? Is the doctor in on this also?"

Rude Buay would rather not discuss his love interest.

"You know as well as I do that in a war like this one ... no one can be trusted. Not even..."

That went over Mendez's head.

Mendez asks,

"Yeah, but how can you help me help you."

Rude Bauy advises.

"Let's take out the Commissioner. Run this operation as we see fit. We can bring in the tanks, the whole infantry...Then it becomes our war and not theirs."

Mendez, liking where this conversation is going, says,

"You're thinking on your feet. Go on."
Rude Buay follows up.
"Pressure these guys to come out of hiding."
Mendez asks,
"What's the payoff?"
Rude Buay is deep in thought. Mendez senses this. He makes his chess move and continues.
"Yes Rude Buay, the payoff? We're in it...to win it."
Mendez aborts that call and dials. He talks into the phone.
"Commissioner, this is Jose Mendez. I must let you know that I'm going to need a substantial increase or I'm pulling my agents out within twenty-four hours."
Baptiste responds.
"Wait a minute..."
Mendez reminds him of this fact:
"Rude Buay works for us. I repeat ...Twenty-four-hours!"
He hangs up.
It's sun up, outside the Commissioner's home, but Richard Baptiste's not happy. He dials Rude Buay.
"Mr. Rude Buay!"
He answers.
"Rude Buay here."
Baptiste, knowing that he can't win this without Rude Buay replies,
"I'm here for you."
Rude Buay, feeling some local support, says.
"Good deal, Commissioner.

If Axel James tries to leave tomorrow, he'll have to get through reinforced surveillance."

Christine strides in. Make-up and hair in place. Commissioner notices her enhanced sensuality. Baptiste hangs up and chases Christine around the room.

26

BANKS, REFRESHED BY THAT CUP of coffee, paces back and forth in the kitchen. The sunlight beams through the glass window. Horns resonate from ships leaving and entering the harbor. Banks discontinues his ambulating and joins Rude Buay at the table, uttering.

"You remember the guy you shot in the chest during the arrest, search, and seizure in Negril?"

"Yes. What about him?"

"Sources close to the Axel team claim that he was the driver involved in the kidnapping of those government officials. He changed his identity after fleeing from Jamaica with Axel. His real name is Ian Baynes." Banks informs Rude Buay.

"Information left out at the briefing don't you think."

"Don't think it was done purposefully. Late Breaking

News, that's all."

Rude Buay reflects on growing up as a kid, always being *late* for school.

He says to Banks,

"Get me the number for a taxi."

"Where to?"

Rude Buay, in an exasperated huff,

"Port Antonio Hospital."

Rude Buay's Pen Phone rings. He picks up. It's agent Scott.

"Any leads?"

Rude Buay, looking for possible reform in his fellow agent, advises,

"Meet me at the Hospital. I need someone I can trust!"

Banks says.

"Call Sam's Taxi!"

Rude Buay dials.

"Will be here in five minutes," says Rude Buay, as he departs.

Rude Buay sees a display of Rastafarian hats with wigs attached inside an illuminated Vendor's Booth. He purchases one. The Vendor puts the hat in a shopping bag. A taxi pulls up. He gets in, with the bag in hand.

The Taxi runs into a roadblock. Several vehicles are held at bay. Boisterous and angry locals protest in a thick Patois dialect. Drug dealers conduct business amongst barricades as if it is highly legal to do what they do. One man, no doubt, fed up with the disregard for the up-keeping of the law, holds up a sign: I AM RUNNING FOR MP.

Rude Buay, sensing trouble, retrieves the hat and puts it on his head. He sticks his finger in his throat and pukes up outside through the window. That outside door gets plastered... Then he lays flat, face down on the rear seat. An MP walks up towards the taxi and asks the driver,

"Where are you heading to?"

He responds in Patois,

"Port Antonio Hospital. Sick patient. The man sick bad, could be poisoned."

The MP covering his nostrils, signals a policeman to let the cab proceed.

The taxi takes off speedily.

Later, the taxi pulls up outside Port Antonio Hospital. Rude Buay removes the hat. Before exiting, he hands the Driver a U.S. $100.00 Bill. The Driver smiles. Rude Buay exits and enters the hospital.

Baynes is wheeled out of E.R. to a room nearby, accompanied by Tamara. Rude Buay notices her but remains unaffected. Always the professional, she is focused on her patient. Agent Scott, just arriving, observes from close by.

Rude Buay moves into Dr. Tamara Ross' space.

"Hello, Doctor."

She glances up and quickly returns towards the E.R.

Rude Buay, continuing,

"When he wakes up, I need a word with him."
Tamara, very curt,
"When he awakes, Rude Buay."
Agent Scott is bewildered. Did they introduce
themselves?
Tamara continues,
"In my professional opinion, he might not wake up,
period. The bullet to his chest came out through his
rib cage, barely missing his aorta. It's also possible
that he could have suffered considerable memory loss
due to a decrease in the blood supply flowing to his
brain."
"Memory loss. Sounds like someone else I know,"
asserts, Rude Buay.
Scott eyes Rude Buay, surprised.
Tamara continues her work.
Meanwhile, in the hospital room, Ian Baynes holds
his breath and assumes the dead fetal position.
Scott, oblivious, draws closer inside the huddle with
Dr. Ross and Rude Buay.
"So you don't think there's any chance...he asks.
A nurse walks out, and echoes.
"TAMARA, TAMARA the patient just died."
"Sorry."
Tamara says to the agents and departs.
Rude Buay steals a backside view of the doctor. He
goes in one direction, while Scott meanders
contrariwise.

27

LATER, RUDE BUAY, driving through the streets of
Kingston in a Hummer, reaches in glove compartment
for his Pen Phone and calls Mildred.

"Miss Simms, this is Rude Buay. Ian Baynes died while
we were at the hospital."

"Did you get any info from him?" she asks.

"Not a thing. I know he worked with Axel back in
Jamaica. He shot at me during the shootout at the Villa.
Also, he was shot during the sting in MO Bay"

He pauses, then continues.

"Plus my source claims that he could have been in the
van when the government officials were kidnapped."

"Who's your source?"

"Why didn't you guys provide us with that
information?"

"If you did not receive it through the... commissioner's

office, it could be a setup; in an attempt to create a decoy."

"If I'm going to continue on this manhunt, I need an entire profile on Baynes. Who he knew, who knew him, where he hung out, everything!" Rude Buay states, bluntly.

"I'll see what I can do. It's up to the commissioner."

"Is he...?" asks Rude Buay.

She responds.

"You're walking a thin line Rude Buay."

Inside the hospital, an African American man wear-ing scrubs and a mask prowls. He is carrying a doctor's bag. He opens the door to Ian Bayne's room, deposits the bag, and disappears.

Ian Baynes, turns in bed and looks around the room. He retrieves his iPhone from under the mattress. Then he pulls out the top drawer. Baynes, slips on a doctor's uniform, along with a stethoscope around his neck. He throws his iPhone into the doctor's bag. Picks up a syringe and dispenser off the night table, and injects himself in the arm with morphine. He disposes the utensils in the trash, and sneaks out of the hospital.

A Taxicab pulls up. Ian gets in. The Taxi drives off.

Meanwhile, Agent Scott and Rude Buay are reviewing maps. Rude Buay, looks preoccupied but tries to mask it.

Scott asks.

"What's going on?"

"Those three Crooks who were arrested during the

Cold hit on the Tempest. I'll bet that they've got the info that we need to wrap up this manhunt."

Agent Scott responds.

"I don't think you'll get it out of them."

"Why not?"

"Fear. Fear that they and their family are getting killed and fed to vultures."

"What if I offered them protection and the chance to live."

"They know that there's nowhere for them to hide."

Rude Buay, measures Scott.

"I'll have to do this solo."

"Why?"

"I've got a hunch, my friend."

Scott, feeling like he and Rude Buay are now full cohorts, asks.

"What's that?"

"Strike, while the iron's hot. Find a Stool pigeon."

Rude Buay, turns to leave.

Scott remarks.

"I thought we were in this together."

"Time will either promote or expose..."

Responds Rude Buay, as he picks up his gun and exits.

28

AFTER ENTERING THE KINGSTON Police Barracks, Rude Buay hands over a document to the Desk Police. He reviews it, gets on the phone and announces, "Bring out Michael Cox!"

Rude Buay comes to an office, with a small desk, a computer, filing cabinets, and some chairs. Cox is seated on a chair in the middle of the office.

Rude Buay surrounds him, the Police look on.

Rude Buay proceeds.

"Michael, my name's Rude Buay. I'm going to ask you a couple of questions. I ask that you be truthful in your answers."

Michael rubs his nose, unsure what Rude Buay wants.

Rude Buay continues,

"Your name's Michael Cox. Born in Bogota' Colombia?"

"I don't speak English."

"Como se llama?"

"Sorry, I don't understand."

Rude Buay, in disbelief, removes his gun, pointing it towards Michael's head.

"Yesterday, when you were arrested on the 'Tempest' in Negril, what were you doing on that yacht?"

"Kill me, I no tell you nothing!" responds Michael Cox.

Rude Buay looks over at the desk police.

Bring in, Sebastian Perez.

The police, remove Michael from the room and speedily return with Sebastian.

Rude Buay wasting no time -

"Sebastian, what's your affiliation with Michael Cox?"

Sebastian replies,

"Who is that?"

Rude Buay punches him hard in the face. He bleeds.

Sebastian whimpers,

"He's my boss."

"How long has this boss-employee relationship been in force?"

'I don't remember."

"Answer the question. How long?" demands Rude Buay.

"As long as I could remember!"

"And how long ago was that?"

Sebastian nervously responds,

"I don't remember."

Rude Buay gives his last words a digestive interlude.

"What were you doing on the 'Tempest' on the day of

your arrest?"

Sebastian is tight-lipped.

"I..."

Rude Buay punches him again.

Rude Buay restates,

"What were you doing on the "Tempest" on the day of your arrest?"

"Sorry, I see nada, hear nada."

Rude Buay says to the desk police,

"Bring in Nigel Davis."

The Police escort Sebastian out of the room and re-enter with Nigel.

Rude Buay shows Nigel a picture of Ian Baynes and asks Nigel,

"Do you know this man?"

"No. It's my first time seeing him."

"Do you know who Ian Baynes is?"

"I've never heard of him."

"What's your affiliation with Ricardo?"

Nigel responds,

"I don't know him."

Rude Buay is pissed. He grabs Nigel by the collar and throws him up against the wall.

Nigel continues,

"Sorry."

Rude Buay punches him mercilessly. Nigel spits out blood.

"He's my boss."

"For how long?"

"I forgot."

Rude Buays' cup of avoidance is filling up.

"How long...?"

"Sorry, I don't remember."

"You've seen a gallows before?"

"Yes."

Responds Nigel,

"Could you see yourself hanging from one?"

Rude Buay gaits.

"How long since you've been an employee of this...?"

"Long time!"

Replies Nigel,

"And how long ago was that?"

"Since..."

"Since when?"

Nigel deliberates.

"Since he bought the yacht."

"Which yacht?"

Rude Buay pressurizes.

"I'm not a snitch"

Rude Buay sensing a victory moves in closer to Nigel-

"Which yacht...?"

"The blue one."

Responds Nigel.

"Was it the "Tempest"?"

Nigel, showing signs of fatigue, says,

"I'm really tired."

Rude Buay not giving in -

"Was it the...Tempest?"

Nigel responds,

"He had two yachts. Yes."

The Police hand a passport to Rude Buay. He reviews it.

Rude Buay asks,

"Nigel, is this your passport?"

Nigel gives it a good look.

"I think so."

Rude Buay discloses.

"This Columbian passport was recovered at your home. It has not been stamped by Jamaican immigration. How and where did you enter the country?"

Nigel hesitates.

Rude Buay punches him hard in the already bloodied right eye. Nigel's vision becomes blurred.

"We came in by airplane at Runaway Bay, and then took a bus."

Nigel pisses on himself. Urine trickles down his trousers.

"You never got this from me, okay."

"Who else was on the flight?"

"I don't remember."

"Think, recall!"

Nigel ruminates and then comes clean.

"Rebecca Herrera."

Rude Buay inquires,

"Ricardo's wife?"

"Yes sir," retorts Nigel

"Where did she get off the bus?"
Nigel reluctantly answers,
"Ocho Rios."
Rude Bauy meanders away from Nigel. He mulls over
and then asks pointedly.
"What else was on the plane?"
"Fifty kilos," replies Nigel.
Rude Buay returns the passport to the Police and exits
like a man on a mission.

29

THE BLACK HUMMER pulls up in Ocho Rios. Rude Buay arms himself strolls out and hastens outside to a large wooden house. With the use of his gun, he blows out the lock and kicks the door in.

Ricardo, dressed in pajamas, emerges from the bedroom with a gun. He shoots at Rude Buay. The bullet misses him. Rude Buay get a few shots off at Ricardo, who jumps through a window in an escape. Rude Buay takes off on foot, in pursuit.

The Foot RACE continues through a dark alley. Coming around a bend, Ricardo cuts through the bushes.

Rude Buay approaches the bend; there's no Ricardo insight. So Rude Buay proceeds with caution.

Ricardo sees Rude Buay go by and shoots desperately at him. Rude Buay dodges the bullet and lies face down, then rolls over on his back, shooting randomly through the bushes. A bullet hits a wall close to Ricardo. The sound deafens him. He grabs his ears with both hands. His gun falls to the floor.

Ricardo recollects himself. Scrambling for his gun, he locates it, picks it up, off-balanced, discharging several rounds, at the now standing, Rude Buay. He misses his target.

Rude Buay returns fire, hitting Ricardo in the chest and uprooting several plants in the process. Rude Buay get a close up look at Ricardo's blood saturated corps.

He returns to Ricardo's house and opens his closet and rummages. He discovers and confiscates twenty kilos of coke. Rude Buay, sends Scott a text message, via Pen Phone, notifying him about Ricardo's massacre.

A Taxi pulls up outside a mansion overlooking Montego Bay Airport. Ian Baynes ambles out. He proceeds inside the mansion.

Axel opens the door and embraces Ian.

Ian hands over the bag. Axel opens it, removes items, and lays them on the table. The living room is packed with Dragon X cocaine.

"Are you ready for battle?"

Asks Axel.

"I've got enough morphine in me."

Observing the cargo, Ian replies,

"Where's Ricardo?"

"At his house. We'll sail tomorrow,"

Responds Axel.

At Banks' partially lit house in Port Antonio, a man dressed up as a black man steps out of a car. He surveys. Then he moves closer towards the house. He removes a gun from under his coat and gets a perfect aim at Banks, who is at his desk reading blueprints.

Maps and high lighters clutter the table, where he sits.

Banks' phone rings. He moves away from his desk and picks up the phone on the wall.

Vehicles drive by, casting beams of light onto the house.

The Man crouches and lies on the stomach.

Banks returns to his desk.

The Man gets up and recaptures his aim.

He discharges several rounds through the window. Banks ducks too late and gets shot in his left arm. All he sees of the intruder is his disappearing shadow. The man rushes back to his car and disappears.

Banks rolls over onto his uninjured side in pain.

Later, Ian Baynes and Axel James meet with Banks' *failed* assassin. He's still masked, however.

Axel hands over an attaché. He opens it, counts the money. Nods. Departs.

Rude Buay's driving back to the hotel. His cell phone beeps. He tunes in and reads this congratulatory text message from agent Scott.

"Glad you got him before I did. Cause I had a bullet in my gun for him." D.S.

Rude Buay savors the moment and scans the radio for a great music station. He catches the fading of *The Harder They Come* by Jimmy Cliff. The RADIO ANNOUNCER breaks in:

"The weather outlook for Port Antonio calls for clear skies, brisk winds of 10-25 knots, with a high of 86 degrees and a visibility of 30 miles. The high tide is at noon. News just coming into our newsroom: Jeff Cyrus aka "Walter Banks", a former Minister of Parliament and broadcaster here at WE FM was shot at his home in Port Antonio earlier this morning. Banks was rushed to Port Antonio Hospital. He remains in critical condition."

Rude Buay calls Banks from his cell phone and gets a busy signal. He turns the steering wheel to the left and U-Turns, burning rubber in the process. The Hummer merges with the flow of the early morning traffic. It later arrives outside Port Antonio Hospital. Rude Buay hurries inside.

He sees a sign reading: NO VISITORS ALLOWED. Rude Buay, ignores the sign and approaches Banks' bedside. Banks' eyes are closed, tubes attached to his arm.

Tamara enters.

Their eyes meet.

She eyes the sign.

Rude Buay forces a smile.

She smiles.
He leaves.

30

AT BANKS' HOUSE, Jamaican police are busily collecting evidence. Blood is splattered everywhere. Rude Buay approaches and engages a plainclothes Officer.

"How did they get inside?" asks Rude Buay.

The Officer points to a shattered glass window.

"Any leads?"

"No one claimed responsibility," answers the Jamaican Police.

"If anything turns up, give me a call,"

Says Rude Buay, who gives the officer a business card, and heads back to his hummer.

Rude Buay answers his Pen Phone.

"Where are you a partner? You heard the news?" Scott asks.

"Yes, looking for answers," Rude Buay responds as he contemplates.

144

"I'll be trying my luck tonight at the dock. Feel like catching a few Jacks?"

Agent Scott responds.

"I'm in the area. I'll meet you there."

Rude Buay, arrives outside Agent Scott's hotel room. He knocks on the door; no one answers. He breaks in using the screwdriver part of his Pen Phone. Rude Buay rummages through the room and discovers an attaché case. He opens it. There's an African American Man's mask on top, underneath, stacks of Jamaican dollars. Rude Buay takes possession of the attaché case. Soon after, Rude Buay leans up against an iron rail at the Negril Dock, leisurely, viewing the coastline through binoculars. A Taxicab pulls up. Agent Scott gets out and steps into Rude Buay's space. Scott extends a hand. Rude Buay accepts. They shake as good buddies do.

Scott observantly asks,

"No fishing gear?"

Rude Buay answers,

"The bait shop has plenty available."

Scott sensing an intensity in his voice asks.

"Any new information on our manhunt?"

"Very little, since Banks' accident,"

Replies Rude Buay.

Scott, sarcastically,

"Yep. He helped us out a lot."

A small ship sails by in the distance. Rude Buay reaches for binoculars and surveys.

Rude Buay remarks,

"Somebody is trying to double-cross us, Scott."

Scott responds.

"Really?"

"Yep." replies Rude Buay.

"But why? We're here to clean up the mess."

'You think it could be Mildred?"

Rude Buay, asks.

"I thought that she was on our team," remarks agent Scott.

"Everyone seems to be until... "

Scott interrupts.

"They say you can never trust a woman."

Rude Buay ruminates.

"Not even Delilah."

Rude Buay resumes.

"You wouldn't sell out... would you?"

Scott, without hesitating, responds.

"You've known me since the first day of training. I wouldn't sell out on you or the administration."

Rude Buay punches him hard in the face. Scott loses his balance.

"Well you just did, partner," reminds Rude Buay.

Agent Scott struggles to get up and does. He successfully lands a punch into Rude Buays' stomach. Scott replies,

"You have no proof, Rude Buay."

Rude Buay gasp for air. Coughs and spits out blood. Scott comes at Rude Buay with a left hook and misses.

"Proof? You've been gone for most of the time. Ever since that shoot out at the Villa, your time card has missed a lot of ink. Your tattoo is the signature of the Dragon Drug Cartel. I've got more."

Rude Buay, punches him in the face.

Scott retaliates.

"You are not my boss. He's..."

"The Cartel?" asks Rude Buay.

Rude Buay, hits him hard with a right uppercut. Then a left jab. Scott falls to the wooded dock thunderously. The attaché case now lays flat on the dock.

Agent Scott looks at the case suspiciously, then at Rude Buay. Rude Buay kicks attaché into Agent Scott's space.

"Open it, Scott." Commands Rude Buay.

Scott hesitates. Rude Buay reaches for his gun and resumes.

"That's all they paid you to be a rat?"

Rude Buay throws a left uppercut at Scott and misses. Scott with a resentful look to that name comes at Rude Buay swinging the attaché. Rude Buay ducks and the attaché' tumbles to the ground behind him. On impact, it opens up, displaying the mask and stacks of Jamaican currency. Scott gets that final look at the contents as Rude Buay shoots him, in the chest.

Scott falls to the ground and kicks several times to his death. Rude Buay picks up attaché, closing it, he heads towards his Hummer.

On his way there, a car approaches, creating a roadblock. Ian Baynes jumps out.

"Put the attaché' down nice and slow, and drop your weapon Rude Buay."

"How convenient. I could not have planned this," states Rude Buay.

Ian releases safety on his gun.

"You've overstayed your welcome, agent Bascombe.

"Says who?"

"Alberto," replies Ian.

Rude Buay hesitates. Ian shoots at him. Rude Buay ducks to the ground. Laying flat on his back, he fires and shoots Ian in the groin. Ian, in pain, tries to get up. Another car pulls up. Axel jumps out from that vehicle and corners Rude Buay.

"Drop your gun and hand over the attaché! Who's paying you to be a pain in my ass, Rude Buay? The U.S. Government? I know that the government of Jamaica cannot afford too," States Axel.

"Why, because you put the brakes on their economy for your benefit and continue to kill innocent kids with contaminated Cocaine?"

Axel releases the safety on the gun. Rude Buay proceeds to comply.

Ian, regaining his composure, demands,

"Your gun, Rude Buay."

Rude Buay, drops the attaché case, spits out blood onto it. He aims the gun at Axel's head. His gun's jammed.

Axel James whacks Rude Buay in the face with his gun. Rude Buay, falls over, then staggeringly gets up. Axel James not trusting him, asks,

"Who's picking up the tab?"

Rude Buay, refuses to enlighten. Axel hits him again. This time, he falls over thundering to the ground. He remains there. Axel removes a rag from his back pocket and sticks it inside Rude Buays' mouth. He removes Rude Buay's shirt and ties his hand behind his back with it.

Axel picks up the attaché' and Rude Buay's gun. He opens the rear door, throws them inside the car. He returns with some rope, which he uses to tie up Rude Buay. First, he ties the rope in his mouth, like a bit in a horse's mouth, then he ties his hands and feet. He drags Rude Buay to the back of the car and throws him in the trunk. He closes it and gets ready to drive off.

Ian heads to his car. Axel, yells out,

"Join me for the Kill!"

Ian accelerates towards his car and opens the rear door. A few blocks away, a white car, speedily approaches, pending a head-on collision with roadblocks. The car stops. Banks gets out with his bandaged left arm and removes the roadblock. He gets back in and drives away. Further up the street, he encounters the same scenario. This time he drives through clearing the obstacle. This time the car spins around with him almost losing control of it. He continues driving, avoiding all traffic signs. Pedestrians dash out of the car's way.

Ian finally locates his bag of weed and then retrieves an Uzi from the rear seat of his car and jumps in the front passenger seat.

Banks car pulls up at the dock.

Walter Banks jumps out. He's just able to get a few rounds off at Axel's disappearing car. He gets back inside his car, and engages in a chase, unable to match the speed of Axel's automobile.

31

A HUMMER PULLS UP outside the Kingston Police Barracks. Mildred jumps out and scurries inside the building. A Jamaican Police Officer pushes his cup of coffee aside and hands Mildred an envelope marked fingerprints report. Mildred enthusiastically breaks the seal and examines the contents.

She says, "Thanks!" and leaves in a hurry.

The informed officer, with his eyes, stuck on her, yells.

"Aren't you going to need some backup?"

"Thanks but I've got it under control from here on in." She darts outside.

Mildred, meets the Commissioner coming in. She hands him the folder. He opens it and reviews the fingerprints report. He cautions.

"You know as well as I know now, that we can't trust Agent Scott."

"I assure you that I'll get to the bottom of it." She

promises.

Richard Baptiste, appreciative of her commitment, declares,

"My job is on the line, Miss Simms! "

Mildred picks up folder and exits.

Mildred jumps inside the black Hummer and drives away.

Banks, previously noticing Rude Buay's car at the dock, maintain a suspicion that Rude Buay is inside that getaway car and continues in pursuit. He reaches into his breast pocket and pulls out his Pen Phone. He radios.

"Rude Buay come in. This is Banks."

There's no answer.

He continues,

"Rude Buay where the hell are you? We've dis-covered the Snitch."

Still no answer.

Banks aborts that call and dials Mildred's number.

Inside the hummer, Mildred picks up. She knows it's Banks.

"Mr. Banks, give me the good news!"

"News? The bad, the good or the ugly? The bad: Agent Scott's body rests at the dock. The Ugly: My car is in shambles after going through two separate roadblocks. The good: I am still looking for him, after having a shootout with Axel and Ian. Rude Bauy's vehicle was there but he wasn't there. I have a strong hunch that they took him captive."

Mildred asks.

"Or where else can he be?"

Banks replies.

"With the doctor."

Mildred is peeved.

"That's impossible." She declares.

Banks, mockingly,

"I'll bet you..."

Mildred responds.

"Did you call him on his pen phone?"

Banks states,

"No response."

"Let me call you back. If you hear from him before I do. Please ask him to call me." demands Mildred

Mildred aborts that call and dials. She is more peeved. She gets no answer and goes on a tirade..

"Rude Buay you need to pick up...You're a ... a disgrace to this country...the U.S. Government, the Deceiving Evil Administration. If this manhunt goes sour, your ass will rot in a Jamaican prison. Pick up or else...You flake."

Mildred stops outside a coffee shop. She gets out and goes inside.

MOMENTS LATER, Mildred sits at a table sipping coffee. Her Contractor walks in. He's dressed in Jamaican police uniform. She motions him to a seat at her table. Mildred surveys, and waits for privacy, then hands him an attaché' case. He opens it. It's loaded with stacks of E.C. Bills. He closes it. Mildred, eyes her Contractor as he leaves and commands.

"Finish her!"

Her Contractor takes off with it in a hurry.

At the Port Antonio Hospital, A tall Jamaican police officer parades the corridor. Dr. Tamara Ross, dressed in blue scrubs delivers a chart to the Nurse.

"Give this medication to Mr. Castello in an hour. Absolutely no visitors are allowed," The doctor admonishes.

The Nurse asks.

"That Baynes guy didn't wind up at the Morgue, huh? Could this be Voodoo?"

Tamara, informs her that:

"The Jamaican police are conducting their investigation."

She smiles deceitfully as Dr. Ross exits.

Crickets are creaking, as Tamara sits on the grass, next to the old breadfruit tree. Burning candles form a periphery around her. She holds up pictures of Mr. Castello towards the heavens. With eyes closed, she meditates.

The Contractor, disguised as Jamaican Police Officer shows up. He surveys. There's no sign of Tamara. He departs.

Back at the hospital, the Nurse is on the phone with Axel. She informs him.

"The doctor has just left for the Botanical Gardens."

Axel is ruffled, he can't stand the thought of the doctor

escaping. He yells at the Nurse.
"Find her and finish her!"

32

WITH NOT MUCH SPACE to move around in the trunk of the car, Rude Buay uncomfortably tosses and turns, trying to break himself free from the ropes.

Tamara instantly receives an epiphany of her purpose in Rude Buay's life. She expediently blows out the candles and gets into her black BMW, driving away speedily. An Unmarked sedan pulls up. The contractor steps out. He surveys for the second time. He returns to his car and drives away.

A White van appears. The Nurse exits, gun in hand. She notices the candle's residue. Upset, she KICKS them over, returns to the white van, and makes a swift U-Turn.

Tamara glances in her rearview mirror as she senses being tailed. She is, so she speeds up.

The Sedan with the contractor tailgates ferociously.

She nervously speeds up as panic sets in deeper and deeper.

The white Van turns a corner. It proceeds illegally in the opposite direction at high speed, focusing on a head-on collision. The Sedan is still in pursuit of the Tamara. Her BMW veers left speedily. The Van crashes head-on with the sedan, killing the Contractor and Nurse instantly.

INSIDE AN UNNAMED SHIP, in a black armchair, wrapped in a white sheet, sits agent Hudson. She has many bruises and concussions to her face and head. Her feet are tied together, with hands tied behind her back and duct tape, fastened over her mouth.

She tries desperately to PRY herself loose. Finally, she manages to break loose of the rope around her legs and makes baby-like steps as she drags the chair she's attached to, closer towards the door. Shelly enters from the deck and notices that Hudson has moved somewhat. She slaps Hudson in the face.

Denise and Agnes run down into the hull of the ship. Shelly slaps her again, grabs her by her hair, and tugs viciously. Hudson's head rocks back and forth complimenting the movements of Shelly's hand.

Shelly warns her:

"Don't even think about it, Bitch. If this happens again, we'll pluck out your ten fingernails, one every morning until..., and then we'll work on your toenails. We'll call

it the "Mani-Pedi-vicious-extract." You hear me?"
Agnes re-ties Hudson's feet tighter. She winches.
Agnes pulls the rope tighter, thus adjusting her stance.
She looks Hudson dead in the eye and declares
boisterously:
"Do you have any idea what it's like living in jail?
Bitch! "
Then she slaps Hudson, twice in the face, and
continues.
"FYI, it stinks like hell; just like your feet.
They drag the armchair with Hudson on it, back to its
original location. This time, Shelly ties agent Hudson's
hair around a pole.
Denise stands to her left, Agnes to her right and Shelly,
facing her, asks,
"Who is paying, to keep Rude Buay in
Jamaica?"
Hudson, surprised to be asked this question, says.
"I don't know what you're talking about."
Denise disagrees.
"She's lying!"
Agnes insinuates.
"You've worked with him for six years. You know how
he squeezes his toothpaste."
Shelly, trying to break her down:
"Tell us. You know he sleeps around."
Hudson responds,
"I'm not seeing..."
Shelly, inquisitively asks.

"Where does he live in Miami?"

"I'm afraid that I don't have the answer to your question," replies Hudson.

Outside on the deck, a lassoed rope dangles from the ship's mast.

Denise reflectively calls Hudson's attention to the rope.

"How would you like to be hung from the mast of this ship tonight?"

Hudson shudders.

A Blonde Woman walks in and hands over a stack of pictures to Shelly.

Shelly browses through the unique collection, asking,

"Who feeds information to Rude Buay from Colombia?"

To this question, she answers,

"I don't know."

Agnes not believing her asks,

"What do you know?"

Shelly agitated by Hudson's avoidance of supplying information, goes into her deep past -

"Bitch, who did your dad pay to take out my MAN in Bogotá?"

"I don't know what you're talking about."

Denise insinuates,

"You got this job based on nepotism, didn't you?"

"Let my dad rest in peace. I've paid my dues."

Shelly shows Hudson a Polaroid.

"Who's this standing next to you?"

Asks Shelly.

"Ross! Dr. Tamara Ross."

Shelly removes a picture of Hudson, Hudson's daughter, Hudson's dad, and Rude Buay from the stack. She shows it to Hudson inquisitively.

"How old is she?"

Hudson refuses to answer.

Agnes fetches the tray with a pair of pliers and lint on it. She lays it on the table in front of Hudson. Agnes looking at Hudson's daughter evokes,

"We can use her as a Mule. Her granddad will tell us."

Agnes gets ready to extract Hudson's nail on her right index finger.

Alberto walks in. Shakes his head.

Agnes changes her mind and slaps her instead.

The three women untie her hair from the pole. They remove Hudson from the chair, bind her from head to foot with a rope, and attach weights to her legs.

Shelly hands a piece of paper to Alberto with Dr. Ross's name on it.

Alberto reminisces,

"We financed her education at the medical school in Grenada. The best in her class."

Then he looks at the clock, reaches for his cell phone, and dials, he's oblivious that Rude Buay is inaccessible.

Rude Buay's Pen Phone rings in the car trunk. He frantically tries prying himself loose.

His Phone rings several times then stops.

33

MILDRED SIMMS GLIDES IN. Her office phone rings.
She answers on the first ring. It's The Commissioner.
"Mildred Simms."
She senses something different in his voice.
"Oh, hi Mr. Baptiste."
He reports,
"The curfew's lifted. Tomorrow the carnival
celebrations will begin under strict supervision."
She jumps up out of her chair. The phone's still off the
hook. She is euphoric -
"Yes! Yes! Yes!"
(singing and dancing)
"It's carnival time again."
The streets of Kingston are teeming with trucks,
carrying steel bands and masqueraders. Buses and
minivans drop off passengers and make U-Turns to

accommodate those waiting to be brought into the city. The sound of steel pan music and calypso fills the atmosphere. People dance and wind up under the heat of the blazing sun. Steve, standing on top of a truck, plays music from his steel pan as a man possessed. Calypsonians and Reggae artists are singing their hearts out. It's masquerading galore! People dance to the calypso beat. The procession continues for several blocks. Music and more music fills the air.

ALBERTO DIALS FROM HIS CAR. Dressed in faded blue jeans, muscle shirt, ostrich boots, and a red bandanna, Salvador, in his mid-forties, of Colombian descent, picks up the phone.

Alberto commands,

"Hold the shipments for seventy-two and a half hours."

Salvador enlightens,

"Boss, too much traffic. Can't get through."

Alberto recommends,

"Instruct the truck drivers to postpone their pick up until after we dock."

Salvador whimpers,

"This cause mucha problema. The police, the police...You know?"

Alberto disapproves,

"What do I pay you for?"

Salvador butters up,

"You know I got your back boss...I fix it."

"Maricon! That's what you said when you used "Cyanide" to cut it."
Alberto chides before hanging up.

A CADILLAC DRIVES UP and stops in Compton, Los Angeles. Several customers rush out into the street, like passengers fighting for a yellow cab on a rainy day in New York City. One bargain hunter gets in and slams the door shut. The Cady takes off.
That Buyer drooling says,
"Can I get a kilo, Holmes?"
The Dealer ponders,
"Only half a kilo, dawg. It's going to cost you the same price as a regular kilo. You know that, right?"
"When is the rain going to fall?" asks the Buyer.
"Who knows? El Nino could be seriously delayed."
"If it doesn't soon, this place could turn into an inferno. Thanks!" he shouts.
He gives the cash to the Dealer. The Dealer hands over his last bag to the Buyer. The Cady stops, the Buyer opens the car door and exits in a hurry. The Cady continues on its way.

SEVERAL WOMEN DRESSED IN SCRUBS, masks, and surgical gloves, holding on to bed-pans wait in line in front of the restrooms at a Jamaican hotel. Teenagers join a line in front of the restrooms. The women serve them a pill and a glass of water. One by one, teens are escorted into stalls by an attendant carrying a bed-pan. Individual flushes follow minutes after each teen's exit. Women exit later carrying a covered bedpan.

Outside the hotel, the jaded kids re-board the bus, accompanied by two tour guides and a Hispanic woman, carrying an attaché case.

The Bus departs.

34

INSIDE THE CAR TRUNK, Rude Buay with his ear to the ground is still lying on his back. He battles against time, as he vigorously rubs the ropes that bind his hands against the metal hinge. Strands of frayed rope increase with the continued rubbing. Beads of perspiration running down his face, and into his mouth. Tirelessly, Rude Buay, keeps trying.

Finally, the rope severs. He rolls over from his back and onto his right side. Rude Buay reaches into his jacket pocket and pulls out his Pen Phone gadget. He proceeds to scan the trunk with it. A diagnostic Light flashes from the gadget. He then uses hands to grope in that direction. The agent tugs on the wire harness and peels away the sealed black electrical taping. He eyes the wires, so many of them; now he's confused.

The car gains altitude, going up a precipitous hill.

Rude Buay clicks on the pen section on the Pen Phone,

and out comes the screw driver portion. He utilizes it, stripping away the blue and then red wires on that wire harness. Now, he's more confused as he tries to decide which wires to unite. He closes his eyes then opens them.

The Car comes to a stop on top of the steep hill. Axel dials Alberto's number, envisioning a "Three Man Execution" of his kidnapper. Rude Buay, unites two wires. The car trunk pops open. He JUMPS out and scuttles down the mound.

Axel James opens the car door, upon noticing the shadows of the split-second movement of the car trunk. He and Ian Baynes release the safety on their guns and rush cautiously towards the back of the car. They look inside the trunk and over the embankments on either side, but there's no sign of Rude Buay. They get back inside the car peeved and speeds away.

Laying beneath the thick shrubbery over the mound, Rude Buay radios from his Pen Phone.

"Banks come in."

He dials from that phone in a hurry. There's no response.

Rude Buay sees a donkey tied to a stake. He unties the animal and gets on for a ride. The donkey begins to gallop and kicks him off. He gets back on, again it gallops kicking him off. He grabs the donkey by its right ear twisting it and forces a rope into its mouth creating a bit. Now controlled, he briskly rides *it* to a distant shack.

At the shack, he notices a wrecked Land Rover parked in the yard. Rude Buay, jumps off the donkey's back and DASHES inside the jalopy. He hotwires it with his gadget. It cranks up. The noise attracts several barking dogs embarking on the property, in investigative pursuit. Rude Buay hit the road inside the vehicle.

35

INSIDE THE UNNAMED SHIP, Alberto waits, staring at an unopened bottle of champagne in front of him on a table. Axle and Ian arrive empty-handed.
Alberto demandingly inquires –
"Where is our MAN?"
Axel James apologetically retorts,
"Boss, we've lost him."
Alberto advocates,
"The girls would not have..."
Axel challenges,
That guy is very slippery...
Ian Baynes interrupts,
That guy is unstoppable...
Alberto vetoing their incompetence -
Shoots Ian Baynes in the head.
"The girls don't think so, pieces of...

INSIDE THE REARVIEW MIRROR, Rude Buay sees a black Hummer approaching. He stops the Land Rover abruptly on the side of the road and jumps out.

Rude Buay quickly removes his jacket, waves it in the air at the oncoming vehicle. The Black Hummer comes to a SCREECHING halt. He retrieves a gun from under his trousers foot and pulls the gun on the female driver. Surprisingly, it's Shelly Hall. The rear doors open. Out jump Agnes and Denise, with guns drawn. Shelly peers into his soul seductively. He feels the penetration but compartmentalizes in exchange for an aim at Shelly's head.

Rude Buay commands,

"Give up Hudson. End this ordeal!" Agnes, previously preoccupied with the white Mini Van parked several yards away, inches up closer toward Rude Buay in protest.

"Not a chance Rude Buay!"

"Stop this drug trade. You are destroying..."

Shelly proposing,

"We need your little Mildred Simms and Banks."

"Why?"

Asks Rude Buay.

Shelly declares,

"They are impeding traffic."

"They're the property of the Jamaican government."

Retorts Rude Buay.

"Help! Help!"

A Voice echoes, from the vicinity of the white Mini Van.

Rude Buay's attention is drawn peripherally to the abandoned Mini Van. The three women's guns remain focused on Rude Buay.

Shelly, goes to the rear of her vehicle and fetches a five-gallon container. She opens it and immediately creates a broad wet gasoline trail leading towards the abandoned vehicle. On purpose, she pours some on Rude Buays' lower trousers and his shoes.

The cry for help coming from the abandoned vehicle intensifies. Denise releases safety on her gun. Rude Bauy, aims at Denise but gazes at the wet trail on and in which he stands.

Agnes moves into Rude Buays' space and whacks him behind the head with her gun. He falls to the ground. Before he could reciprocate, Denise whacks him with her gun. Rude Buay gets up, staggers. His gun is now wet after touching the ground. With one continuous kick, he sends their rifles sailing into mid-air. Their weapons fall back to the ground. Unfortunately, for them, their guns are now wet with gasoline. All four of them scuffle for the wet weapons. The scene turns into an impasse; everyone cognizant of the deadly effects triggered by a little spark.

Inside the Mini Van, Bazil Taylor, one of the tied-up government officials struggles to set himself free. He finally slips his right hand out of the noose.

Meanwhile, Rude Buay inches in closer towards the

abandoned vehicle. He slips, as a result of the incline and gasoline drenched surface. He regains his balance and knocks the pursuing Shelly to the ground. She gets back up. It turns into a fist fight, with Rude Buay gaining the upper hand.

Bazil Taylor is now out of the abandoned vehicle and comes crawling towards them on all fours. His feet are still tied to his right hand. Denise unties the malnourished Taylor and throws the rope to Agnes. Shelly is still engaged in hand to hand combat with Rude Buay.

Agnes catches the rope and twists it into a lasso. She throws it towards Rude Buay's neck and lassos him. She DRAGS him towards the hummer. Despite his fighting tactics, they manage to subdue him and throw him inside the SUV.

Denise grabs the three rifles and puts two in the Hummer. Shelly grabs one from her, dries it off with her red bandana, and jumps out. She gets ready to waste Taylor.

A white car pulls up and makes a swift U-turn. Every second count, realizing that they have Alberto's Man. So she aborts shooting Taylor and boards the hummer. Inside the white car, is the bandaged left arm man, Walter Banks. His eyes connect with the disappearing hummer, driven by Agnes. Taylor steps into view. Banks is not only breathing gasoline but the mud on his shoes is saturated with it.

Banks yells out,

"Mr. Taylor! Mr. Taylor! Mr. Taylor! You are alive! Those idiots."

Banks puts Mr. Taylor in the rear seat of his car. Before leaving the scene he rummages through the abandoned vehicle and discovers the other three ministers of government all tied up, yet still alive. He unties William Russell, Vince Laborde, and Michael Young. He puts them in his car. With a mixture of joy and sadness, he drives away from the scene.

ALBERTO SITS ON THE SHIP'S DECK, across from Axel. Axel focuses on his boss's gun pointing towards him. Alberto removes safety and perfects his aim. Two men, PEDRO and RAPHAEL, dressed in expensive business suits, white gloves, and sunglasses observe.

Agnes, Denise, and Shelly emerge, dragging Rude Buay. Alberto takes away his deadly aim,

Alberto signals Pedro and Raphael. They lift Rude Buay into a semi-upright stance. Rude Buay regains his presence of mind and realizes that he's now faced to face with ALBERTO.

Their eyes lock. The captive audience made up of Axel, Shelly, Denise, Agnes, Pedro, and Raphael looks on.

Alberto interrogates,

"Rude Buay. You've been a thorn in my side. You didn't keep your promise. OUT means I want you OUT."

Rude Buay inquires,

"Where's Hudson."

Alberto retorts,

"Her funeral? You wouldn't attend, Rude Buay."

Rude Buay recaps,

"You've killed innocent people including kids."

Alberto does not bat an eye.

Rude Buay continues,

"You are a menace to the Caribbean and all that it stands for."

Alberto reduces the effect -

"You killed that teenager when you were a kid. Sin is sin. Right? How's the doctor? Are you aware Rude Buay that I've funded her education."

Rude Buay surprised; he does not want to believe what he just heard.

Alberto continues,

"When you think pleasant thoughts of her you should always think of me."

He gets up, circles and punches Rude Buay hard in the face. Rude Buay falls over. He shakes it off and gets back up. Alberto hits him again. This time he stays down. Pedro grabs him and drags him down the steps into the hull of the ship.

There's no one there in the hull, except for tiny droplets of blood, scattered on the hardwood floor. Rude Buay stares at the bloodstains. Before he could bathe in his pain and sorrow, Pedro and Raphael quickly strap him into the same black armchair, previously occupied by Agent Heidi Hudson. Axel and Alberto enter.

Alberto's cold as ice. Stands erect.
Alberto commands,
"If he moves, kill him."
He smilingly says,
"Goodbye Rude Buay! "
Pedro looks at Raphael in agreement. Nods, yes. Axel
and Alberto head off in a hurry.

36

AXEL JAMES GIVES Alberto a tour of the city of Port Antonio. He looks across at his boss, sitting in the passenger seat.

"Boss, Shelly, and Agnes are anxious to join Denise if she would like to traffic again."

Alberto responds,

"Every agency is looking for them by now."

Alberto looks at his watch.

"When does our intestinal shipment arrive?"

Axel informs,

"The LA and Miami shipments have already cleared customs. No word yet on our next local shipment."

Alberto instructs -

"I need an update."

Alberto's phone rings.

Denise Gomez, sitting in her car outside Michael Manley Airport, bites her fingernails. She's not happy.

"Hello," replies Alberto.

Denise reports,

"Pappy! Those three kids got sick and are held in custody at Michael Manley airport,"

"Conyo!" yells Alberto.

Continuing he questions,

"Where are you?"

"Waiting in my car outside the airport."

She replies.

Eavesdropping Axel James discloses,

"Salvador blew it!"

Alberto dials again.

Inside a tent filled with empty seats in Bogota, Columbia. Salvador answers his cell phone.

"Hello!"

" Salvador! I'll kill you and your whole... family,"

Threatens Alberto.

'Que pasa senor?"

"You're selling me out."

"No senor!"

"The kids got busted, Sal."

"I no tell nobody."

"How much are they carrying?"

Inquires Alberto.

"Two kilos senor."

"Overweight! Only one... kilo! "

Alberto frustratingly hangs up the phone, screaming out -

"Maricon! Maricon! Maricon!"

A few blocks away at the hospital, Dr. Tamara Ross, accompanied by her medical team of two Nurses, cuts through Junior Carlos' stomach wall. They remove several tiny packets of cocaine and lay them on a tray. The Commissioner walks in, stares at the tray and then at the patient. He's concerned. Junior Carlos begins to slip in and out of a coma.

One of the nurses checks the intravenous equipment attached to his forearm. It is secured. Tamara checks his pulse. Once, twice, three times. All eyes are focused on the heart monitor. The heartbeat is irregular. It continues to worsen. Finally, he stops breathing.

Tamara looks at the tray and exclaims,

"Tough kid!"

Commissioner Richard Baptiste shakes his head and walks out of the room.

37

BANKS AND MILDRED pull up outside the hotel. Mildred is driving an SUV and Banks is in his banged-up wreck. Several vehicles are double-parked, blocking the narrow street. They jump out and ZIGZAG their way through the cars, in a mad rush towards the hotel lobby.

Patrons mingle, some with drinks in hand. The music reverberates from the room close by. Banks and Mildred push through the crowd. They push open a door leading to the stairway. The intoxicated patrons react to their intrusion. A woman staring at them pulls out her cell phone and makes a call. Then she rejoins the party.

Mildred knocks on Rude Buay's door. There's no response. She fires and blows out the lock. Banks kicks in the door.

An open, half-empty suitcase is on the bed. There's no

sign of Rude Buay. Banks looks in the bathroom, while Mildred looks under the bed. He's not there. On the dresser is a framed portrait of Clifford, Rude Buay's brother, nestled alongside pictures of two ships - "The Tempest" and "Gomez." Banks clues in. They exit and rush through the exit door leading downstairs.

Shelly, Agnes, and Denise drive up. They enter the hotel in haste.

The already frazzled patrons are shoved out of the way by Denise, Agnes, and Shelly. They get onto the elevator, armed to the maximum. The elevator door closes. Simultaneously, the exit door opens. Mildred and Banks exit and rush outside.

They race to their vehicles and depart.

Patrons have gradually vanished, anticipating a showdown. Denise, Shelly, and Agnes get off the elevator, survey, and anger turns into fury. They rush outside. Banks and Mildred are nowhere in sight. They jump into their SUV and travel in the same direction.

Banks and Mildred arrive at the dock. They survey. Banks notices the ship "Ambassador" with a fresh coat of paint. They climb aboard with guns drawn.

Raphael is alerted. He reaches for his Automatic weapon. Just before he can get one-off, Mildred blasts him. He soars overboard.

Denise, Shelly, and Agnes' SUV arrive at the dock. They see Raphael fall overboard. They enter the ship with their weapons drawn.

Inside the hull of the ship, Pedro, responding to the

sound of gunfire, leaves Rude Buay unguarded and goes to the ship's deck.

Pedro encounters Mildred and Banks. He shoots at them and misses. The three women, now on deck, are inching closer on Banks and Mildred's tail.

In the hull, Rude Buay tries hard to pry himself loose.

On deck, Denise, Agnes, and Shelly are now shooting furiously at Banks and Mildred. Banks returns fire, Shelly gets hit and goes down.

Banks turns around and shoots at Pedro, he misses. Denise shoots at Mildred, who goes to the floor, rolls over and shoots back at Denise. The bullet grazes her right leg.

Denise, falling to the ground, shoots back at Mildred, and misses. Mildred gets up in an attempt to get a shot off at Denise.

Denise shoots at her again. Mildred ducks, return to the floor and lies flat on her stomach. Mildred fires and shoots Denise in the leg. Denise accidentally falls overboard.

Rude Buay finally slips his leg out of that noose, with his tied hands.

Banks, at the duel with Pedro, eludes him. Pedro shoots back at Banks, and then at the emerging Mildred in a flash. He misses.

Banks and Mildred reposition themselves, aiming at Pedro, who positions himself in front of the entrance to the hull of the ship. Losing that aim Pedro searches for the perfect one.

Rude Buay cuts his way out of the ropes. He picks up the armchair with both hands and heads towards the steps leading to the deck.

Pedro's attention is focused on Mildred, who continues to rain bullets in his direction. Rude Buay, now nearby, hits Pedro in his back with the chair.

Pedro falls backward into the hull of the ship. His gun falls out of his hand in the process. Rude Buay stands over him with the hoisted armchair.

"Where's Hudson?" Rude Buay inquires.

Pedro looks at him and doesn't reply. Rude Buay strikes him again with the chair.

"Where's she?"

Once again he does not reply.

Rude Buay, hits him again with the chair.

Pedro rolls over, this time he grabs Rude Buays' two feet, attempting to bring him down. Rude Buay stumbles. In the process he picks up Pedro's gun, and shoots him in the chest, killing him.

Rude Buay notices a door to a closed room in the hull. He turns the doorknob, swinging the door ajar. Inside, he discovers dozens of guns, stockpiled, a huge assortment of bullets, along with stacks of grenades in a corner. Additionally, there are two shelves with stacks of cash in various currencies. He grabs two of the guns, checks them to see if they're loaded with bullets. They are. He hurries to the deck, with guns in hand.

Banks and Agnes exchange gunfire. Mildred reloads.

Shelly gets back up, staggering.

Rude Buay EMERGES. Both guns were drawn demanding -

"Drop the gun, Agnes. You're under arrest."

"Says who?"

She responds.

Rude Buay aims at her head.

"Where's Heidi Hudson?"

"I'm not your Bitch's keeper."

"Lead me to her and you'll go free."

"I'm not for sale Rude Buay."

She reaches for the pulley attached to a rope overhead and SWINGS it in Rude Buay's direction. He ducks.

She jumps overboard. Rude Buay dives into the water after her.

Shelly staggeringly regains her presence of mind and challenges Mildred into a fistfight.

Mildred drops her gun and takes her on.

Shelly shows her the "snake". Mildred shows her the "eagle". Banks observes as they go at it "karate style."

One kick from Mildred finally lands Shelly overboard.

Meanwhile, Denise does not resurface.

Rude Buay swims viciously in pursuit of Agnes. He sees her. Agnes somersaults and eludes him.

Shelly dives under, goes after Rude Buay.

Agnes emerges and grabs at Rude Buay's legs.

He senses her move and punches her in the face.

Her head rocks backward, she goes under.

Rude Buay comes up for air and spits out a mouthful of water.

Shelly pursues him. He grabs her by the head and pushes her under. She kicks hard, gasping for air. Agnes resurfaces, and grabs hold of Rude Buay around his neck. He fights her off, thereby releasing his hold on Agnes, who at this point is drinking water like a fish. Shelly resurfaces, fatigued. He PUSHES her under; after she takes in many gulps of water, he releases her.

Jose Mendez, smoking a Cuban cigar observes from the dock. His eyes lock with Rude Buay's.

"Rude Buay, we've got bigger fish to fry. Who's left on board?" Mendez asks.

None of the women resurfaces. Rude Buay considers them drowned. So he climbs up out of water. He notices Mildred carrying two guns. He grabs one of the guns, and points towards the ship. Mendez tips his cigar, releasing some ash.

Mendez commands,

"That wouldn't be a good move Rude Buay."

Rude Buay is preoccupied.

"Still no word on AGENT HUDSON, huh? Rude Buay ignores him and SHOOTS viciously into the ship. Blowing it up into pieces. Mendez looks at Rude Buay with concern and continues.

"Hudson's not on that ship. Is she?"

Rude Buay does not respond. Instead, he looks around and realizes that he has a choice of who he rides with,

Banks or Mildred. He gives both of them thumbs up.
He chooses to ride with Banks in his banged-up car.

They take off, leaving Mendez standing at the dock
with Mildred proceeding in tow.

Rude Buay begins rubbing his nose.

"Thanks. Is your car leaking fuel? And, how did you
find me?"

Banks responds,

"I'll answer the second first."

"Banks, what if someone cut your...fuel line?"

Rude Bauy gets ready to open the car door. In the
rearview mirror Banks notices, as Mildred takes a
detour.

"Relax Rude Buay. You are safe. It dried from your feet
but mine are still wet."

"Fill me in. Enough of the parables. 'When the student
is ready the teacher appears.' "

Banks reciprocates,

"Well, your footprints were at the scene. And if they
finished you off they had to be heading back to sea and
this was the nearest port of escape. Plus Mildred and I,
trying to find you, had to break into your hotel room.
We saw your brother's photo on both ships owned by
the cartel."

"Really... and Mr. Taylor?"

Retorts Rude Buay.

"I took all four of them to the hospital. They were
treated and discharged."

"Four?"

Inquires Rude Buay .

Banks fills him in -

"Russel and La Borde and Young were also in the back of this vehicle."

"Nice work...horse. I mean bloodhound. Great instincts! Dinner is on me. But first I need to stop at the Haddon Hotel."

Banks pulls up outside the hotel.

Rude Buay receives a text message on his waterproof cell phone.

TEXT READS: Received a tip - Alberto is at Sunset Shores. M.S.

Rude Buay says to Banks.

"Wait here. See who shows up. I'll be at Sunset Shores Hotel!"

Rude Buay get out of the car and catches a Taxi.

38

THE SOUND OF THE WAVES creates a musical ambiance for the oceanic backdrop at the Sunset Shores Hotel. Alberto and Axel, sitting in a suite, are joined by Carlos dressed in an expensive suit and dark sunglasses, along with a Blonde Woman. They sit around a table, drinking. Axel takes out a pack of 555 cigarettes from his pocket. He opens it, withdraws five from the box, lays them on the table.

Carlos strips the tobacco out of the five cigarettes, creating a heap.

Axel takes some cocaine from off a plate on the table, sprinkles the base onto the tobacco, creating half and half. He then feeds the cocaine laced tobacco back into the empty cylinders of paper until the cigarettes are three-quarters packed. He twists the unfiltered end creating a closed valve.

Carlos lights a match and holds it under the cigarette to heat it. The cigarette is toasted gradually, as the oil from the base shows through the white paper. Carlos lights the cigarette and passes it first to Alberto. He takes a toke, passes it to Axel, who takes a toke and passes it to the Blonde, who takes a toke and burns her finger while she passes it to Carlos, who takes a toke.

Carlos feeling the buzz looks up at Alberto and asks,

"Don Alberto when do we sail?"

Alberto doesn't respond.

Carlos inquires -

"Manana?"

Alberto finally pays him some attention asking -

"Did you tie her down properly?"

Carlos is high as a kite.

"Si don Alberto."

The Blonde Woman intercepts -

"I didn't see him put holes in the ship."

Alberto winks at Axel. Axel pulls out his gun and shoots Carlos in the face.

The place becomes a bloody mess.

"Let's get out of here!"

Commands Alberto Gomez.

"Where too?"

Asks Axel.

"Hudson knows too...much,"

Responds Alberto.

Alberto's phone rings. He answers,

"Hello!"

It's Shelly and Agnes.

"Alberto, the Ambassador has been destroyed. Rude Buay has once again escaped. He was last seen at the dock with Banks and Mildred. Your wife Denise is missing. She could be feared dead."

"Where are you?"

"Heading to Sunset Shores,"

Responds Shelly.

Alberto hangs up. He is not happy.

39

A TAXI DRIVES UP at Sunset Shores Hotel. Alberto, Axel, and Blonde Woman get in. The taxi drives to the Port Antonio dock. Alberto JUMPS out of the cab. He's FURIOUS.

Axel and the Blonde Woman exit the cab staring at the remains and simultaneously at their boss. Alberto sees a Catamaran speed boat docked on the other side. He heads in its direction. Axel and the Blonde Woman follow in Alberto's tracks.

With guns drawn, Alberto, Axel, and the Blonde Woman climb aboard. Three people: Tommy, Margaret and their teenage daughter Niki sit around a table enjoying a lobster dinner.

Alberto, Axel, and Blonde Woman move in. Before the family could take flight, bullets start raining on them.

Bullets hit Tommy and Margaret, who soar over-board from the impact. Niki runs for cover. Axel follows Niki.

Alberto reminds Axel -

"Spare her, she's a hot commodity!"

Axel refrains from shooting her but maintains his aim.

Axel heads into the cabin and cranks up the engine.

The Blonde Woman, playing team, runs ashore, loosens the rope which ties the ship to the dock, and makes her way back on deck. The Ship sails.

The Blonde Woman seeks out the teary-eyed Niki. Axel releases his aim on her and throws her a Snicker bar. Niki, scared, but deprived of her dinner, take a bite. The Woman reaches into her pocketbook, retrieves a hairbrush, and gently styles Niki's hair into a ponytail. Niki dries her tears. The Woman grabs some rope, attaches it to Niki's hair, and ties it to the mast.

Alberto is busy scanning the shores through a pair of binoculars.

 Catamaran KICKS up white water.

 SHELLY, DRIPPING WET at a phone booth, dials in a hurry.

"I need a taxi at Hope Bay Terrace."

Momentarily, a taxi drives up. Shelly pulls the driver out of the taxi and places him under a chokehold, and pops his neck. The Cabbie falls to the ground to his death. Agnes comes out from behind the tree and takes the wheel, while Shelly accesses the front passenger seat. The Taxi drives away.

Shelly calls on Cabbie's cellular phone which she found inside the taxi.

Alberto's cell phone rings. He picks it up.

Agnes responds.

"We're heading to the Sunset Shores Hotel. Is our man there?"

"He's waiting for you. Hurry,"

Replies Alberto.

BANKS ENCOUNTERS PROBLEMS as he tries to get a signal on his laptop, outside The Haddon Hotel. Finally, he does, as he picks up video of Shelly and Agnes getting inside the taxi. He discovers that it was not in real-time. He catches up to speed and overhears their phone conversation.

Banks gets Rude Buay on the phone.

"Rude Buay, Shelly and Agnes just left the beach. They are heading to the Sunset Shores Hotel."

Rude Buay replies,

"Cover the Sunset Shores Hotel. I'm heading there too."

Banks arrives and waits in his car. A taxi pulls up. Shelly gets out and enters the hotel. Agnes continues the ride.

Banks picks up his phone and dials Rude Buay.

"Rude Buay, Agnes dropped Shelly off in a taxi."

"Did you get the tags?

"Yep. The license tag is H 29562. She's driving that thing like a maniac."

Rude Buay responds,

"Keep an eye on Shelly. Do not let her leave the hotel."

Rude Buay's car accelerates through the crowded night street. The Cab in question, leaves, heading in the opposite direction.

Rude Buay's SUV immediately makes a swift U-turn, in pursuit. Shooting at the taxi, he deflates the rear tires. The taxi slows up. Rude Buay hit it again, shooting Agnes in the neck.

The car collides into the wall, bursting into flames.

Rude Buay departs.

His Pen Phone rings.

Banks, on the other end, discloses,

"Rude Buay, Shelly just walked into the hotel. She's alone."

"Great! Hold on."

Rude Buay reviews a text message which he received earlier from an informant. On that list is the name Carlos Chavez, a guest at Sunset Shores Hotel.

"Banks, I need the profile on... Carlos Chavez."

Banks goes to work and pulls up the info from his laptop's database.

Banks discloses,

"A Former DEA, worked alongside two of your superiors, Bob White and Jose Mendez. He moonlighted as a prison guard, busted for cocaine possession in 2002, a master in disguise. He has a

Miami address. Do you need it?"

"No. Awesome! Call the commissioner, ask him to send in backup."

Rude Buay responds as he pulls into the Hotel's parking lot.

In the hotel room, Shelly, almost unclothed, bruises on her body, rolls out of bed. She glances at her lover in bed, lying on his stomach. She strides to the bathroom.

Before getting out of the car, Rude Buay radios Banks. "Banks I want you to stay put. I'll call you if I need you."

"What's up with that, are you a loner?"

"DEA business!"

Rude Buay meets his informant in the lobby and gives him a wad of cash. He hands Rude Buay a slip of paper with the room # 122.

Rude Buay moseys up to door. Disregarding the hanging no disturb sign. He aims at the lock with a silencer attached to his gun, and fires, blowing out the lock.

He kicks in the door.

On impact, Shelly darts out of bed, and grabs a gun from on top of the dresser, along with her lover's bulletproof vest. The man turns over in bed. A close up reveals him. It is Special agent Jose Mendez. Rude Buay is oblivious. He scuttles out of bed, turns off the lights and seeks refuge in the adjoining vacant suite.

Shelly hides behind the dresser. She pulls her blouse over the vest.

Rude Buay enters, gun in hand. Shelly accidentally bumps into the dresser.

Rude Buay fires, a bullet penetrate the dresser and grazes against Shelly's gun holding hand. She loses control of it. The gun hits the floor. She's off balanced and tries to regain her presence of mind while lying on the floor. She succeeds and retrieves gun. Getting up she shoots at Rude Buay. He returns fire.

The bullet misses her as she hits the floor behind the dresser.

Meanwhile, bullets from other room come flying at Rude Buay. He turns in wonderment. Shelly shoots again. Rude Buay dodges and fires back at Shelly as he gets up. The bullet strikes Shelly in the chest, knocking her to the ground.

Rude Buay stares at her in admiration but shoots her again in the chest. She kicks a few times. Rude Buay thinks that he has taken her out with that last shot. Rude Buay hears the front door to the adjacent room open. He rushes through the front door to the hotel room.

He locates a light switch, turns on the light and peeps inside the adjoining room. It is empty. Peripherally he notices a shadow. He turns and gets a glimpse of a man's shadow going around the corner.

Rude Buay pursues the shadow, still ignorant of the performer's identity. As Rude Buay carefully grazes the wall, you can HEAR a pin drop.

Suddenly, he hears the sound of a gun reloading. It sounds just like his. Rude Buay checks his gun and proceeds with caution.

Mendez is now moving closer towards Rude Buay, in the same proportion as Rude Buay is moving towards him. If it wasn't for the 90 degree wall between them they would be shaking each other's hand.

Rude Buay gets off a random shot. So does Mendez. The shadows of their outstretched hands on the wall alert them to the tiny distance existing between both of them.

Rude Buay hugs the wall with the gun in his right hand and fires. The Bullet misses Mendez's ducking head.

Mendez purposefully goes flat on his stomach, gun in hand as he aims, waiting for Rude Buay to turn the corner.

Walter Banks, coming up the stairs, darts through the exit door, with gun in hand. He sees the perpetrator's backside. The man is lying flat on his stomach with his gun pointed in the opposite direction. The Exit door closes after Banks's entry. Rude Buay is alerted. Banks yells out,

"Rude Buay! Hold your fire. I've got him cornered!"

Mendez, responding to both sounds, rolls over on his back and shoots at Banks. The shot misses him. Rude Buay appears around the bend and yells,

"Banks, don't shoot! He is mine!" Mendez is still facing Banks with his back turned to Rude Buay. Rude Buay, still uncertain of the man's identity, commands -

"Turn around you... prick!"

Mendez, sensing that two guns are now pointing at him, turns slowly. He is now facing Rude Buay, who castigates -

"Suit? Lies! Deception! Duplicity! Sabotage!"

"We're on the same team, Rude Buay."

"We are?" asks Rude Buay.

"We've always been."

"Really? Where's Hudson?"

"You should be answering that question, Rude Buay... You turned her over to Alberto. She stood in your way." Mendez responds.

"Which way?" inquires Rude Buay.

"Your promotion. You brought her to the Caribbean so that you could orchestrate her kidnapping." responds Jose Mendez.

Banks eyes Rude Buay and then Mendez. Not trusting anyone, he's aiming at both men. Is this what I came out of retirement for? He reasons.

Mendez continues,

"How much did Alberto pay you and how much more did you agree to pay Carlos Chavez for all of this?"

"Nice try. You know what, Boss? You stand in the way of my promotion. So I'm going to have to cap you. Then I'll find Alberto and cap him. Then..."

"Do you think that Alberto is going to fall into your trap. You'll never catch him. He's invincible," Interrupts Mendez.

Rude Buay aims at Mendez's head, motioning him to

get down on his knees. He does.

"If you kill me, the parasites that devour my body will tell me. You'll never catch Alberto."

Rude Buay retorts,

"The record states that You've killed off several Colombian Officials in the 1990s and gave Alberto Gomez control of the most vicious Colombian Cartel. Etched his name and signature. Claiming that it will be so hot. All five oceans wouldn't be able to cool it."

Rude Buay continues,

"Off the record, I'm about to release that DAM, Jose. Drop your weapon!"

Mendez shoots at Rude Buay, and misses. Rude Buay fires, shooting Mendez in the head. Mendez kicks and stops breathing. Rude Buay confiscates his gun. Looking at it, he declares,

"In every arena, there's a need for great teams. Men and women would become champions if they committed to playing team."

Rude Buay and Banks make a B-line to inside Shelly's hotel room.

They rummage through the room. Rude Buay discovers an attaché case with the initials: JM. He pries it open and throws everything out on the bed. He delves through the contents, while Banks observes.

List of recovered items:

1. A shotgun

2. A pair of binoculars.

 3. A miniature camera.

Pictures of:

1. Rude Buay and Tamara cuddled up on the beach.
2. Rude Buay struggling with Shelly in the water at the dock.

Rude Buay notices Axel's name on the back of one of Mendez's business cards with phone number 876-362-0800 Ext. 27.

He hands it to Banks.

Banks responds instantly,

"This Hotel!"

They throw the evidence back inside the attaché. Toting it along, they leave in a hurry.

Rude Buay and Banks approach room # 27. A no disturb sign hangs from the doorknob. Rude Buay blows out the lock with a bullet. He enters, followed by Banks in tow. They react to the strong stench. Lying on the ground soaked in blood is Carlos Chavez. There's a gunshot wound to the head. Rude Buay rolls him over and discovers the dragon tattoo behind his right ear. A flashing infrared light directs Rude Buay to a cell phone inside Carlos's breast pocket.

Rude Buay removes the phone. Their attention is then drawn to the four-chair dining table. On it lies the residue from a free-basing session. Banks collects the leavings.

Rude Buay toys with Carlos' cell phone. First with the camera wallet. Several thumbnails exist. Rude Buay searches through the pics.

Pic # 1: A close up of Warden Culligan's corpse.

Pic # 2: The Ambassador.

Pic # 3: Warden Ralph Bullock's house.

Pic # 4: A close up of Warden Ralph Bullock.

Pic # 5: Agent Hudson bound with ropes in a dinghy.

Rude Buay goes to a full screen on the thumbnails. Next, he accesses the phone book. Two phone numbers for Alberto Gomez pops up. Rude Buay dials the first one. There's no answer, so he tries the second number.

"Hello, this must be good news!"

Answers Alberto.

The sound of a boat's engine and that of waves splashing against a huge object is heard in the background.

Rude Buay quickly hangs up. He exits, departing with Walter Banks.

An SUV pulls into the driveway, followed by Jamaican police. Mildred steps out, almost colliding with Rude Buay and Banks.

Mildred articulates,

"The hotel called saying that you were on the premises. Where's Axel?   Is he finished?"

"We're about to find out," Replies Banks.

Several Jamaican police cruisers with flashing lights have blocked the entrance to the driveway making it a hazardous exit.

Mildred jumps inside Banks' jalopy. It is fully loaded with wiring and gadgetry. Jamaican police officers, already having entered the building on foot, return, responding to tooting horns. They clear the entrance of parked police cruisers. Rude Buay manages to turn his car around speedily. They drive away at top speed to the dock.

The two cars pull up parking precariously. They jump out, proceeding hurriedly on foot.

A Native administers some serious elbow grease as he polishes a blue and white 400 SuperSport speedboat.

Rude Buay demands,

"DEA, we need to use your boat."

The Native looks at him like he's crazy.

Mildred supplicates,

"Come on! We'll return it."

The Native, checking out Mildred's physique articulates,

"Not even my wife gets behind this wheel..."

Rude Buay pulls out his gun on the native exclaiming

"This is a rescue mission. We don't have time to explain. Don't make me have to force you to..."

The Native disembarks.

Rude Buay, Mildred, and Banks jump in.

Banks grabs the wheel. The boat takes off careening between other ships at the dock.

Native yells,

"You return it one scratch...mon you'll be...dead meat!"

In afterthought, he continues,

"It's almost on empty! "

Rude Buay asks,

"What did he say?"

Mildred holding on tightly to the rail answers,
" Something like...don't bring it back on empty. His
patois is awful."

40

THE 400 SUPERSPORT picks up speed as it travels through the waters of Jamaica's north coast. A Jamaican police helicopter follows overhead.

Inside this speedster, Rude Buay and Mildred scan the coast with aid of binoculars. Rude Buay answers to the ringing of his Pen Phone.

It's The Commissioner.

"Rude Buay, we've given you all that we've got available. "

Rude Buay looks up in the distance, acknowledging the helicopter.

"The man found dead at the dock was identified as sailor Tommy Clarke and his wife Margaret, owner of the missing Catamaran. Autopsy results indicate that they could have been killed less than thirty hours ago," Informs The Commissioner.

Rude Buay rejoins Banks who's enjoying the machinery.

"They could have already made their escape to Colombia. They have got a huge head start on us. How fast can this thing go?

Banks looks at the gauge meters, showing signs of uneasiness.

"What's the fuel capacity on this...?"

"It says, two hundred and fifty gallons," Indicates Rude Buay, after which the fuel gauge grabs his attention.

" It's on empty. So is the reserve tank."

He continues,

"Where can we refill?"

Mildred walks in, binoculars in hand, comments,

"Are we really on empty?"

"We're eight miles from land,"

Indicates Walter Banks.

A ship heading in the opposite direction passes nearby, leaving a trail of water, causing a huge undercurrent. The SuperSport gets caught up into that current, creating maneuvering problems for Banks. Rude Buay and Mildred grab onto the rail to avoid losing balance. Mildred informs,

"Making this stop is going to cause us to lose those bastards. I want Axel's head served up on a... platter."

Rude Buay responds,

Would that make them the property of the Colombian

government?"

"They could refuse to release them to us,"

Banks cautions.

"How much faster can this thing go?" Banks asks, with Cuba now close-in view.

Rude Buay replies,

"The faster we go. The more fuel this rocket consumes. Inside the Jamaica Helicopter overhead, the pilot adjusts his binoculars stating,

"We've spotted the Catamaran off the coast of Cuba."

"There's not enough time for us to refill in port,"

States Rude Buay.

Banks radios,

"400 SuperSport heading south, five miles off the Island Cuba, requesting assistance! Running low on fuel. I repeat: We're running low on fuel."

Suddenly the engine stops and the boat begins to drift. In Port Antonio, a Pickup truck pulls up at the wharf. The Jamaica Helicopter, circles overhead. Two natives hurriedly secure the laden gas container inside of the helicopter's lowered net. The Copter takes off in assistance.

The Copter attempts to lower the container unto the 400 SuperSport. Rude Buay tries to grab it. High tide creates treacherous waves causing the ship to drift from underneath the descending net.

Copter flies right, making another attempt. Another wave rocks the ship further right, making that drop off more difficult.

Meanwhile, the Catamaran picks up considerable speed heading north. Axel helms the ship, while Alberto and the Blonde Woman engage in a free-basing session on deck. Niki observes. Two Automatic weapons resting in the men's arms extend onto the table. Looking through his binoculars, Alberto spots a dinghy adrift in the distance. His curiosity increases as he zooms in for clarity.

"That could be Hudson!" he remarks.

The dinghy's passenger continues waving a portion of a sheet to the distant, rapidly approaching Catamaran. The 400 Super Sport continues to drift briskly further as the waves continue to rise higher and higher. The Copter comes in for its third attempt. Before the depositing of the container on board the 400 SuperSport, the Co-Pilot notices the catamaran, up ahead, traveling at runaway speed.

The Pilot unites the net with the 400 SuperSport. Rude Buay fetches the container and immediately starts the refueling process.

The Helicopter's Co-Pilot reaches for his pair of binoculars. He sees not only the Catamaran in the lenses but the dinghy, sailing away, with someone in it, waving a large piece of fabric.

He reports -

"We've spotted the missing Catamaran cutting water towards Cuba. There's someone in a dinghy ahead of it, waving for help."

Rude Buay FIRES up the engine and takes over the wheel.

Mildred joins Rude Buay in the helm seat. She is armed with her 350 magnums.

Banks survey the coast from the cockpit, binoculars in one hand and gun in the other.

The SuperSport begins CUTTING water at an increase of speed.

The Catamaran continues sailing at a step it up speed.

The Helicopter up above progresses with increased velocity.

Axel draws Alberto's attention to the dinghy still drifting at sea. A woman's image is now visible. The Blonde Woman onboard the catamaran grabs a pair of binoculars and zooms in. Realizing that it's Heidi Hudson she exclaims -

"That bitch is still alive?"

The sound of the approaching helicopter, changes the mood, as three binoculars are tossed aside in exchange for automatic weapons. Alberto, Axel, and the Blonde are now engaged in a shootout with (a) the helicopter pilots, (b) firing simultaneously at the dinghy. Niki tries desperately to untie herself from the mast. The Blonde Woman notices her planned getaway and aims at Niki yelling,

"Don't you dare."

Niki retreats. The Catamaran's engine is *turned* off.

The tide favors it and it pulls away from the 400 SuperSport still trapped in its rapids.

The Dinghy continues to drift. Gunshots begin to rain down onto the Catamaran from the Helicopter overhead. The exchange of firepower continues. Axel and Alberto retreating with several rounds. None of these bullets make contact with the helicopter though. Moving full speed, the 400 Super Sport's gaining momentum on the Catamaran.

The Catamaran is now in a comfortable shooting distance from the supersport. Rude Buay, Mildred and Banks proceed with the onslaught. Several bullets ricochet onto the Catamaran.

A Bullet from Mildred's gun hits the Blonde woman, explosively. She hits the deck hard. Her breath dissipates from her body.

Axel and Alberto return fire onto the 400 SuperSport, missing everything but the water.

The Dinghy with the lone, tired, sunburnt agent Hudson, is now in close view.

Alberto shoots at her. The Dinghy rides the huge wave causing him to miss, but puts a gaping hole into its left side.

Water begins to seep through, filling up the dinghy. Hudson is discombobulated.

A helicopter swoops down, lowering its net for agent Hudson. She reaches the net like it was the last straw, amidst the continued shooting between the DEA agents and the two drug lords. She is unsuccessful.

Axel gets back to helming the Catamaran, speedily. He desperately tries to create some distance between it and the SuperSport.

Rude Buay returns to the helm seat.

The 400 SuperSport picks up speed, in pursuit. The swift movement of the water, enhanced by the water current caused by both ships, washes away the dinghy, as soon as Hudson successfully grabs onto the net. The Helicopter briskly departs from the area with agent Hudson holding onto the net. Alberto shoots excessively at the rescued agent Hudson. He misses his target as he competes with the wind's trajectory. Rude Buay continues to shoot at Axel and Alberto from the helm seat. Banks moves to the bow, in an attempt to secure his stance. He is off-balanced but shoots desperately at Alberto, who's stationed in the Catamaran's cockpit.

Several bullets from Alberto's gun intended for Banks strikes the 400 SuperSport, damaging it. Banks retaliates with several rounds.

Bullets severely penetrate the Catamaran. One of the bullets brushes against Alberto's leg. He's off-balanced. More bullets rain, hitting the Catamaran's mast, grazing close to Niki.

"No. Please! No!"

Screams Niki.

Niki's screams aren't heard. Rude Buay, Mildred and Banks are oblivious that she is aboard. They continue to shoot aggressively at Alberto and Axel.

A huge wave pushes the Catamaran out of focus. Bullets from the 400 SuperSport miss that ship. Alberto returns fire. A Bullet from his gun hits Banks in his left upper arm. He goes down. Mildred runs to his aid. He's still breathing. But aching severely.

Rude Buay evens the score, blowing out several portholes. A series of waves rock the punctured Catamaran. Pushing it closer to a "run ashore" collision on the Island of Cuba.

Axel emerges with Niki as his human shield. A huge wave hits the Catamaran.

Niki screaming hysterically,

"Don't kill me! You son of a bitch!"

Mildred eyes Rude Buay as he aims for Axel's head. The movement of the boat makes it tough to maintain the focus of the bullet's trajectory.

Axel points his Automatic weapon towards Niki's head. Her screaming intensifies.

Rude Buay emerges closer on deck. He, eyes Mildred assuredly. He shoots. Instead, a bullet from Axel's gun hits Rude Buay in his chest. He falls onto the deck.

Mildred keeps dodging Axel's bullets. Rude Buay with blood on his vest, rolls over onto his stomach and gets a good aim at Axel. Discharges.

The bullet HITS Axel right between his eyes. He falls backward thunderously onto the deck. Niki falls forward into the deep.

A mountain-like wave beckons. It hits the Catamaran viciously. Alberto, dressed in a wet suit jumps over board into the wave, unnoticed by everyone on the other ship. The Catamaran sails speedily towards an unavoidable collapse onto the island of Cuba.

Mildred dives into the deep, and clutches Niki around her neck. Rude Buay throws out the life rope. Mildred catches it. Rude Buay reels them in.

Another mountainous wave hits the Catamaran, it slams into Cuba at full speed, bursting into flames, debris, spikes, and fragments of lumber.

THE HOSPITAL LOBBY IS CROWDED with Jamaican police officers. Banks is pushed around in a wheelchair with his left arm in a sling. The Police commissioner, Mildred, and Rude Buay admire compassionately. Rude Buay walks up to Banks and hands over an attaché. Banks opens it. He smiles upon seeing the stacks of crisp C notes. He closes the attaché, gives Rude Buay a thumbs up and departs. Agent Hudson walks out from the discharge room, accompanied by Tamara. Rude Buay greets agent Hudson smilingly. They turn to leave.

Richard Baptiste steps into their space, and utters -

"Thanks, Rude Buay."

"My pleasure,"

Says Rude Buay.

Tamara rushes past the commissioner, right into Rude Buay's space. Their eyes become locked momentarily. Mildred moves closer towards Rude Buay, scrutinizing her.

"Rude Buay, you forgot something," says Tamara.

"My vest!"

She flies into his arms. Mildred eyes them enviously.

ALBERTO STANDS OUTSIDE the Medical School in Grenada dressed in an expensive business suit and dark glasses. Clipboard and pen in hand urging -
"Sign up for educational funding!"
Several enthusiasts form a line in response.

SHELLY AND DENISE JUMP INSIDE a waiting Jamaican taxi.

ABOUT THE AUTHOR

John A. Andrews, screenwriter, producer, and author of several books, founded Teen Success in 2009. Its mission statement: *To empower Teens in maximizing their full potential to be successful and contributing citizens in the world.* As an author of books on relationships, personal development, and vivid engaging stories, John is sought after as a motivational speaker to address success

213

principles to young adults. John makes an impact in the lives of others because of his passion and commitment to make a difference in the world. Being a father of three sons propels John even more in his desire to see teens succeed. Andrews, a divorced dad of three sons ages 14, 12 and 10, was born in the Islands of St. Vincent and the Grenadines. He grew up in a home of five sisters and three brothers. He recounts: "My parents were all about values: work hard, love God and never give up on dreams."

Self-educated, John developed an interest in music. Although lacking formal education he later put his knowledge and passion to good use, moonlighting as a disc jockey in New York. This paved the way for further exploration in the entertainment world. In 1994 John caught the acting bug. Leaving the Big Apple for Hollywood over a decade ago not only put several national TV commercials under his belt but helped him to find his niche.

His passion for writing started in 2002 when he was denied the rights to a 1970's classic film, which he so badly wanted to remake. In 2007, while etching two of his original screenplays, he published his first book "The 5 Steps to Changing Your Life" Currently he's publishing his fifteenth volume, while working on empowering teens worldwide.

In 2008 he not only published his second book but also wrote seven additional books that year, and produced the docu-drama based on his second book, *Spread Some Love (Relationships 101)*.

See Imdb: http://www.imdb.com/title/tt0854677/

"Ask not what your country can do for
you - ask what you can do for your
country."

- John F. Kennedy

www.famousquotes.me.uk/speeches/John_F.../5.htm

FOR MORE ON
BOOKS THAT WILL ENHANCE YOUR LIFE ™
Visit: **A L I**
www.AndrewsLeadershipInternational.com
EMAIL US
www.JohnAAndrews.com

*Rude Buay is a drug prevention chronicle about teens caught up in the war on drugs and contains content for adults; parental discretion is advised for children.

RUDE BUAY ... THE UNTOUCHABLE